CD-R●M
and
Other

Optical
Information
Systems

Implementation
Issues for Libraries

CD-R⬤M
and
Other

Optical
Information
Systems

Implementation
Issues for Libraries

by Nancy L. Eaton, Linda Brew MacDonald,
and Mara R. Saule

ORYX PRESS
1989

The rare Arabian Oryx is believed to have inspired the myth of the unicorn. This desert antelope became virtually extinct in the early 1960s. At that time several groups of international conservationists arranged to have 9 animals sent to the Phoenix Zoo to be the nucleus of a captive breeding herd. Today the Oryx population is nearly 800, and over 400 have been returned to reserves in the Middle East.

Copyright © 1989 by
The Oryx Press
2214 North Central at Encanto
Phoenix, AZ 85004-1483

Published simultaneously in Canada

Printed and Bound in the United States of America

∞ The paper used in this publication meets the minimum requirements of American National Standard for Information Science—Permanence of Paper for Printed Library Materials, ANSI Z39.48, 1984.

Library of Congress Cataloging-in-Publication Data

Eaton, Nancy L., 1943–
    CD-ROM and other optical information systems : implementation issues for libraries / by Nancy L. Eaton, Linda Brew MacDonald, and Mara R. Saule.
        p.   cm.
    Bibliography: p.
    Includes index.
    ISBN 0-89774-448-9
    1. Optical storage devices—Library applications.   2. Optical disks—Library applications.   3. Optical publishing—Library applications.   4. Information technology.   5. Libraries—Automation.   6. CD-ROM.   I. MacDonald, Linda Brew.   II. Saule, Mara R. III. Title.
Z681.3.O67E28 1988   88-29385
O25.3′0285—dc19   CIP

Contents

List of Figures

Preface

Optical (laser) disc technology has burst onto the library scene within the last three years, introduced and celebrated by the industry as the next major breakthrough in information technology. The preface to Microsoft's landmark publication *CD-ROM, the New Papyrus* (1986) calls CD-ROM "a revolutionary information storage medium, much as was papyrus when it replaced stone, clay, and wood as surfaces on which early Egyptians recorded significant events in their lives." Information industry consultants such as Julie Schwerin of InfoTech and Link Resources, a publisher specializing in forecasting of the electronic-information market, were projecting in 1985 that CD-ROM would be used heavily by libraries within two years and that libraries would be one of the early specialty markets for optical publishing.

The first commercially available product aimed specifically at the library market, Library Corporation's BiblioFile (CD-ROM discs of Library of Congress MARC cataloging records), was exhibited at the American Library Association's midwinter meeting in January 1985. It created a great deal of excitement, but sales were slow. At the June 1986 ALA annual conference in New York City eighteen months later, Library Corporation was announcing a subscriber base of only 250. By July 1988, the subscriber base had increased to 1,200 installations. In the interim, over fifty publishers or vendors had announced CD-ROM, digital videodisc, or write-once products, either in prototype or as actual in-production products. Thus, it is clear that this is a rapidly expanding though still very new information medium for publishers, vendors, and libraries alike. It is especially important that librarians, who are expected to be some of the earliest users of these publications and products, understand the new media and work closely with the information industry in developing publications and products that are truly sensitive to the market they are to serve.

An important question which the library field should begin to address is: Which technology for which applications? Optical media (CD-ROM, CD-I, digital videodisc, write-once, erasable) are among a variety of information delivery methodologies. On the continuum is paper, microform, electromagnetic disk, audio formats, video formats, and optical formats. As the use of electronic recording media is expanding and replacing a percentage of the paper or microform publications, proportional use of all the media is changing. Most likely, all of these formats will continue to be utilized; what will change is the "mix."

The enthusiasm for electronic delivery of information is a response to its flexibility. An immense quantity of information can be stored on electromagnetic disk drives or on optical discs. Electronic information can be transmitted over distances rapidly and downloaded or printed at the other end. It can be searched in a variety of ways which paper or microform publications do not allow. And it can be updated rapidly.

Even with these attributes, electronic storage media cannot be marketed effectively without comparable developments in user software, telecommunications networks, and microcomputer work stations. There must also be an adequate number of microcomputers in the user environment to make electronic publishing economically viable. Recent developments in software, telecommunications, and work stations have paralleled the technical development of optical media. Thus, many of the components that are required for electronic publishing to increase and flourish appear to be coming together.

With the growing number of microcomputers, commercial end-user search systems (both online and optical), online library catalogs, ever-cheaper disk storage for mounting other databases locally, and telecommunications options, user behavior is changing. Users themselves are trying out electronic mail and searching online or optical disc systems. Telecommunications networks allow access from home, office, or library. End-user software is simplifying search logic for direct searching by patrons.

Thus, we must address several important questions:

- What information should be in national online databases, for considerations of either access or economics?
- What information is most useful in local online databases, over in-house or campus networks?
- What information is most appropriate to the new optical disc technology on dedicated in-house work stations or systems?
- How can libraries structure these services and integrate them into existing services so that they make sense to the library patron?

It is the objective of the authors that this book provide a framework within which librarians can begin to address these questions. This book is intended to serve as a basic, self-contained overview of optical technology as it applies to library systems and services. The first chapter reviews the basics of optical (laser) technology at a level sufficient to understand vocabulary and basic concepts. Subsequent chapters are specific to optical technology as it may be employed in the library and information arena, focusing on those issues most critical to the implementation of these systems within the ongoing operation of the library. Chapter 8 presents a discussion of various policy issues that electronic publishing poses for the library and for information professionals, in the hope of encouraging broad discussion and imaginative approaches to these very complex information issues. The final chapter presents selected case studies of libraries that have gained experience with optical systems in operating environments. The authors would like to express their appreciation to those librarians who were willing to share their experiences with colleagues. Finally, the appendices provide a list of producers and distributors of optical products and a selective bibliography.

Chapter 1
The Basics of Optical
Information Technology

Most users of information systems are not interested in optical technology for its engineering elegance, but rather for how it can be used to gain access to information. Thus, this chapter is intended to provide only enough information to convey the general concepts of how optical systems work, to describe the components of optical systems, to make the reader comfortable with those concepts, and to define some of the terminology and jargon which accompany any new technology.

AN OVERVIEW

Optical (laser) technology is a means of capturing information in electronic form by using a light beam to burn microscopic pits into a photosensitive disc surface. The recording tracks can be either a continuous spiral, as on a phonograph record, or concentric circles sliced into sectors, as on a floppy disk. The spiral-recording technique is called CLV, for constant linear velocity, and allows for more efficient use of the disc surface because it packs the data more tightly. But it is sequential and thus can be slower for locating data. The sector-recording technique is called CAV, for constant angular velocity. CAV spreads the data farther apart on the outer rings, resulting in fewer data on the disc surface; however, this technique makes it is easier to locate data on a section of the disc because it is not organized sequentially.[1] Each of these methods of recording affects the software designs used for data retrieval and the time required to locate and retrieve the data from the disc (see Figure 1).

With both CAV and CLV, information is read off a disc by a disc drive which reflects light off the disc surface; the drive's "read head" interprets the pits and lands (spaces between pits) and the transitions between pits and lands according to the variations in the

Figure 1: Representation of CAV and CLV

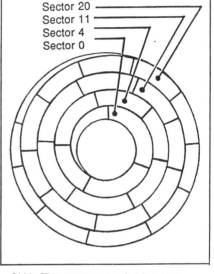

Track 0, Sector 1
Track 1, Sector 0
Track 0, Sector 0

Sector 20
Sector 11
Sector 4
Sector 0

CAV: The sector organization of a typical CAV (constant angular velocity) magnetic disk. The sectors on the outer tracks are physically longer than those on the inner tracks and are organized in concentric rings.

CLV: The sector organization on a CLV (constant linear velocity) CD-ROM. Since all the sectors have the same length, the longer outer "tracks" contain more sectors. Note the spiral appearance of this organization.

(Reprinted by permission from Bill Zoellick, from his article "CD-ROM Software Development: Beware of 'Magnetic-Disk Think', *BYTE 11* (5) (May 1986): 178)

reflected light. The disc drive converts these variations in reflected light to corresponding digital data which is usable by a computer.

Optical discs belong to three general families: read-only-memory, write-once, and erasable. Within each family, data can be recorded in one of two formats, analog or digital. "Analog" and "digital" refer to the types of signals used. An analog signal is the same type of signal used for television and is a wave-like signal. "Digital" refers to the on/off electrical pulses used in computer technology. An analog signal is more efficient for storing motion or graphics in their original form, but has the disadvantage of having to be converted into the on/off pulses of the digital format in order to be used by a computer system. A digital signal is more efficient for computer use because it can be used in its original form; however, it is less efficient for graphics, because the pictures have to be digitized into grids of dots, called bit-mapped images, which simulate the graphics. Digital formats only recently have been able to represent motion, and those formats are very new and still basically in prototype. Thus, analog technology is more proven for use with motion or graphics, whereas digital technology is more efficient for applications that are mostly data or text. Research into data compression techniques for efficient storage of motion and graphics in digital form is ongoing, in order to make digital technology more applicable to multimedia uses.

Of the three optical families, read-only-memory discs cannot be changed once produced. The technology requires that data be sent to a mastering facility and processed onto a master glass plate, which is then used to produce copies that are encased in a clear, very durable plastic. Write-once and erasable discs are recorded directly at the work station. Write-once discs cannot be changed once recorded, though new data can be added following the already recorded data. Erasable discs can be changed and are therefore sometimes called write-many discs. Erasable discs promise greater storage densities than current magnetic storage but with the same flexibility of allowing the user to change the information. Read-only-memory discs and write-once discs are in actual use and available commercially, whereas erasable discs are still under development and not yet available commercially.

TYPES OF OPTICAL MEDIA

Optical discs and associated disc drives combine the various formats and characteristics described above. An optical disc drive is a computer peripheral, just as the floppy disk drive is a computer peripheral. Primarily, these drives are used with microcomputers, though use is projected with minicomputers and mainframe computers for decentralized access to large databases from multiple terminals or work stations on shared telecommunications networks. The various optical disc formats that are being used in information-based systems, their attributes, and their current development status are described here briefly (see Figure 2). For additional information on the technical attributes of the different optical media, articles by David C. Miller and James B. Williams and a special issue of *BYTE* are recommended.[2]

Digital Videodisc

The digital videodisc, also called laserdisc or laser videodisc, is a variant of the entertainment videodisc used for movies. It stores sound, color, and full motion on the videodisc in analog format, and it can carry encoded digital data for use with a computer. Thus, it is a superior format for mixed media (combining sound, motion, color, and data) as compared to current CD-ROM technology. CD-I and DVI (see below) purport to handle motion and color, however, and may ultimately prove the better formats.

Figure 2: Optical Media by Categories

	ANALOG	DIGITAL
READ ONLY	Digital videodisc	CD-Audio CD-ROM OROM CD-I CD-ROM/DVI
WRITE ONCE		WORM DRAW ODDD CD-PROM Lasercard
ERASABLE		CD-EPROM DataRom

Digital videodisc is a 12-inch (30-centimeter) disc, read-only-memory, CLV/CAV format, with information encoded in analog format. It can store one gigabyte of information per side, equivalent to 5 million pages of text or 54,000 video frames, which is almost twice the storage capacity of a CD-ROM, a possible virtue for very large databases. Videodisc also has the capability of random frame access for interactive programming. The encoding formats and file formats are non-standard; thus, discs cannot be exchanged from one information supplier's system to another. It is in actual use with existing products, unlike CD-I and DVI (which have been announced by Sony and RCA, respectively; as yet no existing products have reached the marketplace). The most commonly used digital videodisc player system is produced by LaserData.

CD-Audio (Compact Disc–Audio)

Originally developed by Philips and Sony for the entertainment market, CD-audio is designed for digital representation of music. A CD-audio disc drive is attached to a stereo system in the same way as a turntable. The standards for formatting the information on the disc are described in the Philips/Sony "Red Book" specifications, so nicknamed because the standards were bound in red. The success of the CD-audio discs has made production of other versions of CD more cost-effective; the same manufacturing plants can be used, and thus they benefit from economies of scale.

CD-ROM (Compact Disc–Read Only Memory)

The Compact Disc-Read Only Memory (CD-ROM) is a variant of the audio compact disc used for stereo recordings. It is a more efficient storage medium for digital data than videodisc because it does not have to translate from analog format to digital format, and vice versa, as it interprets data; the data are captured in their original digital format. The disc, a 4.75-inch format, is small enough that its drive may fit into a floppy-disk-drive slot on a microcomputer.

CD-ROM uses a constant linear velocity spiral track; thus, speed of retrieval of data depends upon designing retrieval software that minimizes the CLV format limitations. A CD-ROM stores 550 megabytes of data (excluding file overhead); it can store text, audio, graphics, and software, but not motion, though it can store step animation. It includes error-correction techniques, and a logical file standard is in the process of being accepted industrywide, to facilitate use of a CD-ROM disc on any disc player and with any retrieval software. Storage of graphics is less efficient than as an analog signal, though compression techniques are being developed to improve storage of graphics on CD-ROM. At present, color is converted to gray tones.

CD-ROM has emerged as the leading medium for electronic publishing for material that consists primarily of data with few or no graphics. It lends itself to reference data, library catalogs, and similar data-oriented products.

CD-PROM (Compact Disc–Programmable Read Only Memory)

Announced by Philips in 1986, this product is in the research and development stages. It is a format compatible with CD-ROM, a "writable" compact disc—read only memory that would allow users to copy information from a CD-ROM disc. CD-PROM will require its own drive; it will retain the same physical dimensions as audio CDs, CD-ROM, and CD-I, potentially allowing it to run those other formats on its drives. CD-PROM is not expected to be commercially available until 1988 or later.[3]

CD-I (Compact Disc–Interactive)

Philips International announced the Philips/Sony CD-I standard at Microsoft's First International Conference on CD-ROM in 1986 as its approach to providing motion video for compact disc applications. CD-I is a standard, as opposed to a chip set that can be added to all personal computers and CD-ROM systems. The CD-I standard is a set of specifications which delineate color coding for all television-set formats. These specifications are being added to the CD-ROM file format standards, so that any manufacturer or software producer can design products based upon these standard manufacturing specifications. Using a CD-I disc will require a CD-I player. The standards, however, allow use of the disc on any manufacturer's CD-I drive. It is anticipated that the CD-I drive will also read CD-ROM discs and CD-PROM discs. Philips has announced plans to introduce CD-I hardware in the second half of 1988, later than expected because of delays in the availability of key CD-I components.[4]

Both CD-I and DVI are aimed at the consumer or educational/training markets which require a digital, multifunctional, multimedia product. Production of these products is an expensive enterprise, as it requires scripting, sound, color, and possibly animation and simulation. An estimated production cost for a CD-I master disc is $200,000–300,000.[5]

CD-ROM/DVI (Digital Video Interactive)

At Microsoft's Second International Conference on CD-ROM in Seattle (March 3–5, 1987), General Electric/RCA announced and demonstrated a prototype of a new device called DVI (digital video interactive). In essence, DVI is a peripheral to a CD-ROM disc drive and microcomputer that permits the addition of full-motion video, three-dimensional graphics, and multitrack audio on a CD-ROM disc. DVI is a compression/decompression system for digital video and audio. It has the ability to display one hour of motion video from compressed digital data stored on a single standard CD-ROM disc. To operate DVI, which is a chip set mounted on a special microcomputer board, the user will need (1) a personal computer, (2) an add-on video board, (3) an add-on audio board, (4) the DVI board, and (5) a CD-ROM drive.[6]

OROM (Optical Read Only Memory)

This technology, which has been announced by Sony, exists only on an experimental basis or with proprietary systems. It uses sectored tracks (constant angular velocity) rather than spiral tracks (constant linear velocity) and therefore is purported to produce faster retrieval and response times. Storage capacity is one gigabyte for the 12-inch disc and 250 megabytes for the 5.25-inch disc. At present, there are no standards for data or file structures, nor are there any existing products on the market.

WORM (Write Once, Read Many)

Unlike the read-only-memory (ROM) technology, in which data are sent to a manufacturing plant where a master disc is created and then used to stamp copies for distribution, WORM technology allows the local computer system to write directly onto the disc; once written upon, the disc cannot be changed. Thus, the acronym, from the phrase "write once, read many." It is also called "DRAW," for "Direct-Read-After-Write." The system can continue to add information serially to the disc. WORM discs are available in 12-inch, 8-inch, and 5.25-inch diameters. The 12-inch disc holds 1.2 gigabytes of information per side. Reliable manufacturing of WORM discs came about only in 1987, and distribution still is limited. Use is projected to center around office automation and desktop publishing; it will serve as a replacement for microfilm archives and work as a master disc to create databases, from which copies in small numbers (fewer than ten) or in other formats can then be made.

Optical Card (Lasercard)

The Lasercard, produced by Drexler Technology, is a credit-card-sized unit which utilizes WORM (write once-read many) technology. The strip on the card holds 2 megabytes of data. Because of its portability and because it can be added to serially to update information, it is projected for use with identification cards, for security systems, parts catalogs, medical records, bank cards, digitized maps, technical manuals, and updates to read-only-memory systems. It may also have application for electronic versions of books which can be used with small portable readers.

ODDD (Optical Digital Data Disc)

ODDD is a write-once technology projected for use with minicomputers or mainframe computers in the storage of very large data files. It would provide much denser storage than the electromagnetic disk drives currently in use, but with the tradeoff of slower access and longer retrieval time. ODDD (also called ODD for Optical Data Discs) is in development or proprietary and not yet generally available.

Erasable (or Multiple Write)

Still under development and not yet on the market, this technology is magneto-optical. It will have greatly increased optical storage densities, and it will be erasable like current magnetic media. It is expected to be available in both 12-inch and 5.25-inch discs. Used with microcomputers or mainframes, it would greatly increase the ability to store, access, and update large databases.

DataROM

An erasable product under development and announced by Sony in 1987, DataROM would allow for permanent storage on one side of the disk—similar to CD-ROM—and erasable or write-once storage on the other. This is not expected to be commercially available until 1988.[7] This would allow for updates on the write-once portion to supplement the fixed data on the read-only portion between updates to the CD-ROM. At present, some vendors create the same effect by using a CD-ROM drive and a hard disk drive in combination, but two different drives are required and each has to be searched separately.

CD-EPROM (CD-Erasable Programmable Read Only Memory)

This acronym refers to a version of compact discs that would have the attributes of programmability and erasability. The technology is still under development and not available commercially. Little is known about its prospective design or projected uses.

In spite of all the activity in technological development implied by this complex mix of optical discs, as of early 1988 only three were being used in actual production systems available on the market to information consumers: digital videodisc, CD-ROM, and WORM (see Figure 3). Thus, the remainder of this book will concentrate on the systems and products using those three types of optical discs, since other products are very speculative in the immediate future.

DATA PREPARATION AND DISC PRODUCTION

Digital videodiscs and CD-ROM discs must be mastered and copied (stamped), and those copies used on the actual disc drives. The diagram below describes the steps involved in the production of a CD-ROM by 3M. A similar process is used for production of digital videodiscs. This manufacturing process includes the distinct stages of data capture, data conversion, premastering, mastering, and replication (see Figure 4).

Figure 3: CD-ROM, Digital Videodisc, and WORM Discs

FEATURE	CD-ROM	VIDEODISC	WORM
SIZE	4.75"	12"	12", 8", 5.25"
CAPACITY (1 megabyte = 3 floppies = 500 pages)	550 megabytes	1 gigabyte	12" = 1.2 gigabytes 5.25" = up to 800 mb
MEDIA	Limited (no motion)	Mixed (including motion video)	Limited (no motion)
# OF USERS	Single	Multiple	
STANDARDIZATION	Hardware only (not file format or interface)	None	None
ERROR CORRECTION	Yes	No	No
APPLICATIONS/ EXAMPLES	Bibliographic/Text SilverPlatter Library systems BiblioFile Hybrids DIALOG On-Disc	Bibliographic/Text InfoTrac Training Entertainment	Office automation Desktop publishing Archival storage

Figure 4: Data Preparation and Disc Production

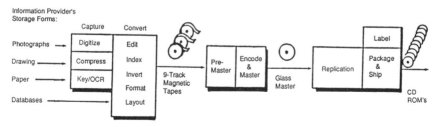

[Adapted with permission from ONLINE, based on a diagram in Nancy Herther's "CD-ROM Technology: A New Era for Information Storage and Retrieval," *Online* 9 (6) (November 1985): 25]

Information may originate in various forms, for example, as text on paper, as drawings, or as an electronic database from the publisher's own in-house production system. If on paper, the information must be either keyed into a computer system or scanned by optical character recognition (OCR) or a similar system and converted to electronic format. Once in electronic format, the stored information must be edited, indexed, and laid out in a format acceptable to the manufacturing system. These data are then copied onto 9-track magnetic tapes or WORM discs and sent to the manufacturing plant, where in the premastering process the data on the 9-track tapes or WORM disc are prepared for the production process and error-detection encoding is added; the data representation is then burned onto the glass master, from which the copies are made.

It is easy to see that the cost of capturing the information in electronic format may be very high. Keying of data by terminal operators is labor-intensive. Thus, optical-character-recognition technology is evolving to make this stage more efficient. Systems by the Palantir Corporation and by Kurzweil combine scanning technology with microcomputer software to create an "intelligent recognition engine" which converts scanned bit-mapped images to ASCII digital code, which can then be indexed and formatted for computer manipulation.[8] Scanners still have a high error rate on many kinds of printed material, such as graphs, tables, and formulas. If automated data-capture-and-conversion techniques are improved upon and have a more acceptable error rate, human editing can then be reduced and can in turn reduce the costs of converting data for large retrospective collections. So long as data conversion remains labor-intensive, libraries and publishers will shy away from conversion of large retrospective files. One demonstration project which will test the Palantir system for data conversion is the National Agricultural Text Digitizing Project, a cooperative project among 43 landgrant libraries.[9] Until scanning technology is reliable in quality and in error detection, most products will be relatively current materials. This desire to capture current information electronically as it is created is the motivation behind the publishing industry's efforts to establish a standard for accepting authors' manuscripts in a standardized, machine-readable format.

A number of companies have emerged to aid publishers and information producers with the data capture and conversion process. Examples are Scientific Applications International Corporation (SAIC), Online Computer Systems Inc., and SilverPlatter. These companies contract with publishers, libraries, or government agencies to help set up scanning facilities, help with file definition, define indexing file formats, and prepare data for the premastering process. Larger publishers or information providers (such as OCLC, Dialog, Wilson, and Bowker) are beginning to build this expertise in-house; but smaller publishers will prefer to contract for this support.

The interlinking relationships between information producer, software support services, disc manufacturers, and work station component manufacturers are represented in Figure 5.

Figure 5: Interlinking Relationships

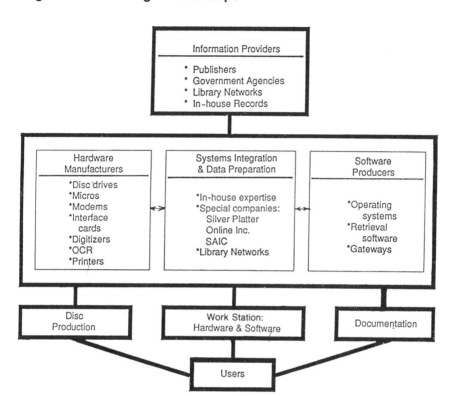

Until 1986, almost all of the final discs were manufactured in Europe or Asia. Since then, many new plants have opened in the United States. Nancy Herther listed fourteen new manufacturing facilities as existing in the U.S. in 1987, as compared to one in 1986.[10] Production turnaround has been reduced to 28 days, though shorter turnaround can be provided at a higher cost. In 1987, SAIC quoted a mastering fee for CD-ROM of $7,000, with an average per disc cost of $10, excluding the cost of creating the content.[11] However, costs are continuing to decline. By June 1988, Discovery Systems announced mastering services for $1,500 and disc replication for only $2 per disc![12]

THE ROLE OF STANDARDS

The development of standards is important because it allows flexibility. The user can purchase equipment from any manufacturer and have it plug-compatible. Standardization thus reduces costs by encouraging competition. It also allows the information provider to develop disc products for a variety of disc players, thus broadening the market opportunities. Finally, standards should make use of the technology easier, as equipment and software incompatibilities and differences in operating procedures are minimized.

Three types of standards are emerging for optical technology: (1) disc standards; (2) drive standards; and (3) interface standards. Standards for retrieval software are unlikely to find industry acceptance in the near future, since the design of software is an area where one vendor can produce a better mousetrap—and thus capture a larger part of the publications market sector. As the number of products and the variety of search software increases, however, users likely will apply pressure on producers to agree upon at least a basic set of search protocols to minimize confusion as the user moves from one product to another.

Disc Standards

There are two distinct kinds of CD-ROM disc standards: physical recording standards and logical organization standards. Disc physical recording standards specify how many data blocks there are, how long each block is, where timing and error codes are recorded, etc. Philips and Sony specify these standards, and evaluators can take them for granted. The Philips/Sony "Red Book" defined physical standards for CD-audio in 1980; the "Red Book" standards have been accepted as the physical standard for CD-ROM as well.

The Philips/Sony "Yellow Book" for CD-ROM addresses volume and file structure and has been extended by the work of the High Sierra Group and the NISO [Z39] Standards Committee EE. Disc logical standards cover the way CD-ROM information files are organized and reported to the drive and microcomputer operating system. The High Sierra Group, an ad hoc group of industry leaders who recognized the need for standardization in this area in order to have broad user acceptance of CD-ROM products, submitted a draft set of standards to the National Information Standards Organization, which expects to finalize the standard by August, 1987.[13]

Philips's "Green Book" for CD-Interactive is in draft form, and the High Sierra Group is trying to incorporate the requirements for CD-I into the CD-ROM standards.[14] For a full discussion of the evolution of the standards for CD-audio, CD-ROM, and CD-I, the Schwerin book provides an excellent historical perspective, as well as a technical discussion of the CD-ROM standard. The *Brady Guide to CD-ROM* provides readable technical descriptions of the "Red Book," "Yellow Book," and "Green Book" specifications.

Drive Standards

Drive standards specify how the drive interprets the disc formatted information. Ideally, any disc can operate on any drive which uses the High Sierra Group disc standards. However, to date there are still some incompatibilities, and users may wish to use the drive recommended by the producer of the disc to avoid such problems.[16] The Microsoft Extensions will help solve this problem; the Extensions are a widely distributed implementation of the High Sierra Group specifications for the popular MS-DOS microcomputer operating system. The MS-DOS operating system interfaces to mass-storage devices and peripherals such as serial and parallel ports through special programs called device drivers.[17]

Interface Standards

Interface standards describe the interconnections or "interface" between the disc drive and the microcomputer. An interface named SCSI is emerging as the microcomputer/CD-ROM drive interface standard. SCSI is becoming the interface of choice between micros and a variety of peripheral devices, such as printers, modems, etc. SCSI includes a number of CD-ROM-drive-specific commands; it also handles many routine chores without tying up the microcomputer.[18] Figure 6 summarizes the total production process for CD-ROM and illustrates the role that each type of standard plays in the hardware and file layout scheme.

WORK STATION COMPONENTS

The work station that is used to retrieve information from an optical disc is a microcomputer with a variety of peripheral equipment attached. Although configurations will vary from one information producer to another, a typical stand-alone work station may include the microcomputer, a printer, an interface card for the printer, an optical disc drive (e.g., CD-ROM, WORM, digital videodisc), an interface card for the drive, a graphics card (if graphics capability is provided), and a modem for exiting to online systems for more current information (see Figure 7).

In addition to the peripherals, the work station and optical disc must utilize various types of software, such as operating systems and retrieval software. This software may be resident on the optical disc itself or provided separately on floppy disks. Because retrieval software is still undergoing significant refinement by most producers, it is more common for the software to be provided separately on floppy disks and loaded into the microcomputer. This simplifies distribution

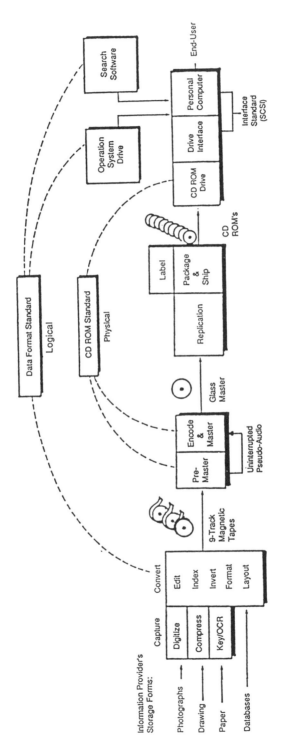

Figure 6: Relationships between Standards

[Adapted with permission from *ONLINE*, based on a diagram in Nancy Herther's "CD-ROM Technology: A New Era for Information Storage and Retrieval," *ONLINE* 9 (6) (November 1985): 25]

Figure 7: Typical Work Station Components

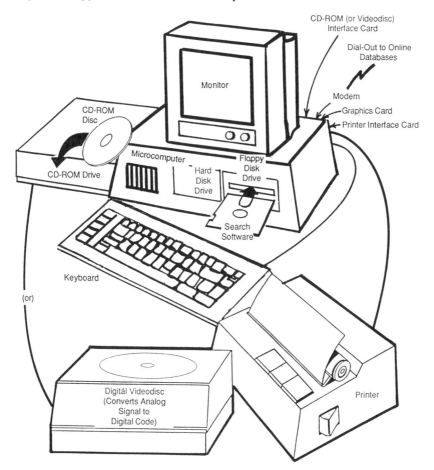

of software enhancements, but it complicates the daily operation of the system if the system goes down and has to be "rebooted" or brought back up, or if the software disk has to be handed out to patrons along with the associated optical disc.

Increasingly, optical work stations are being configured to aid users in switching into online packet-switching networks for searching of online databases. Typically, the user will search the in-house optical database, such as a CD-ROM database. If he or she needs more current information for the same database, he or she will then exit the optical database and select the telecommunications network and online database. A modem and system/telecommunications software aid the user in making this transition. Such configurations are considered in more depth in chapters 3 and 6.

REFERENCES

1. Zoellick, Bill. "CD-ROM Software Development: Beware of "Magnetic-Disk Think." BYTE *(11)* 5 (May 1986): 177–178.

2. Additional discussion of the technical aspects of the various optical media can be found in the following:
BYTE; *the Small Systems Journal* 11 (5) (May 1986) [The entire issue is devoted to optical storage technology.]
Miller, David C. *The New Optical Media in the Library and the Academy Tomorrow.* A Special Report to the Fred Meyer Charitable Trust. 1987. [Available from David C. Miller, DCM Associates, Post Drawer 605, Benecia, CA 94510.]
Williams, James B. *Optical Publishing and Higher Education: The Promise, The Risks, The Issues.* A Special Report to the Fred Meyer Charitable Trust. 1987. [Available from Hypermap, P.O. Box 23452, Portland, OR 97223.]

3. Herther, Nancy K. "CD-ROM and Information Dissemination: An Update." *ONLINE* 11 (2) (March 1987): 58, 62.

4. "Philips Gives Green Book the Green Light" *CD-I News* 1 (6) (April 1987): 3.

5. Rosen, David. "Interview: Gary Kildall, President of KnowledgeSet." *CD-I News* 1 (6) (April 1987): 7.

6. Rosen, David. "GE/RCA Announces DVI." *CD-I News* 1 (6) (April 1987): 1, 4–5, 8–9.

7. Herther, 62.

8. Stanton, Tom; Burns, Diane; and Venit, S. "Page-to-disk Technology: Nine State-of-the-Art Scanners." *PC Magazine* 5 (16) (September 30, 1986): 128–177.

9. University of Vermont and State Agricultural College. Contract with Science Applications International Corporation, under the Cooperative Agreement between the University of Vermont and the National Agricultural Library for the National Agricultural Text Digitizing Project. 1987.

10. Herther, 58–62.

11. University of Vermont.

12. "Discovery Systems Announces Pricing Breakthrough for CD-ROM," *Information Today* 5 (6) (June 1988): 28.

13. National Information Standards Organization [Z39] *Report on the April 13, 1987 Meeting, Gaithersburg, MD.* A memorandum from Martin Hensel, chair, standards committee EE (May 4, 1987).

14. Schwerin, Julie B. *CD-ROM Standards: The Book.* Oxford, England: Learned Information, Ltd. and InfoTech, 1986. 14–15.

15. Buddine, Laura, and Young, Elizabeth. *The Brady Guide to CD-ROM.* (New York: Prentice-Hall, 1987), pp. 355–421.

16. Miller, David C. "Evaluating CD-ROM's: To Buy or What to Buy?" *DATABASE* 10 (3) (June, 1987): 36–42.

17. Ziechick, Alan L. "Extending MS-DOS." *CD-ROM Review* 3 (2) (March/April 1988): 42.

18. Miller, 37.

Chapter 2
An Overview of Library Applications

Optical information technology has been described as a technology in search of an application. Both digital videodisc and CD-ROM technologies are spin-offs of the entertainment industry. The economy of scale had to be provided by the entertainment sector in order to make the technology affordable in the information sector. Thus, though the technology has great potential for information storage and retrieval, it preceded any expressed need in the information sector. As a consequence, information providers are still experimenting with how best to apply the technology, discovering the economics of information products, exploring what has to be done to make the technology a useful tool for users, and testing library and consumer receptivity.

Early applications in the information sector have tended to be spinoffs of print publications or products already in machine-readable formats that can be reutilized for optical publications. For instance, there are now three different versions of the ERIC files available on CD-ROM from SilverPlatter, Dialog, and OCLC. MEDLINE is available on CD-ROM from at least a dozen different information providers, including SilverPlatter and COMPACT Cambridge. BiblioFile is a CD-ROM version of the Library of Congress MARC cataloging records.

New applications are emerging, however. This chapter summarizes the applications that will be most pertinent to libraries. The libraries, products, and vendors named are illustrative only. A more complete list of vendors and products is provided in Appendix A. In-depth discussions of public services and technical services implementation issues are presented in chapters 3, 4, and 5.

As indicated in chapter 1, only a few of the optical media are out of the research and development cycle and available commercially. The applications described in this chapter utilize one of three optical mediums: digital videodisc, CD-ROM, or WORM technologies. CD-

ROM is becoming the *de facto* standard for distribution within the publishing industry. A few products, such as the early InfoTrac, the LaserFile cataloging system from Library Systems and Services, Inc., and the Library of Congress optical disc project with motion pictures and graphics, utilize digital videodisc. Even InfoTrac is now available in a CD-ROM version, however. A perusal of the products listed in Appendix A shows the predominance of CD-ROM as the medium of choice.

PUBLIC SERVICES

Bibliographic Databases

Bibliographic databases are particularly appropriate for publication in optical formats. They benefit from the value-added capabilities of key-word and Boolean searching, and they tend not to have graphics as part of the text. If the databases do include graphics, the graphics are usually omitted in the CD-ROM version of the publication. Because they are citation-based, the retrieval software does not have to provide for the problems associated with full-text retrieval—searching unstructured language out of context.

It is only natural that the first optical products developed for the library marketplace were bibliographic databases, such as Library Corporation's BiblioFile, SilverPlatter's ERIC and PsycLit, and Information Access Corporation's InfoTrac. Since the emergence of those three products in 1985, the number of reference-oriented citation databases has grown to a substantial list, including such products as Bowker's Books-in-Print Plus, Books-in-Print/Out-of-Print Plus, and Ulrich's Plus; the Compact Cambridge series in the medical and life sciences; Datext business databases; DIALOG OnDisc ERIC; Compact Disclosure; SilverPlatter's A-V ONLINE, AGRICOLA, Ca-CD, CHEM-BANK, CIRR, COMPU-INFO, EMBASE, ERIC, LISA, MEDLINE, NTIS, OSH-ROM, PsycLit, and sociofile; OCLC's Search CD450 series; Information Access Corporation's InfoTrac, Government Publications Index, LegalTrac, and Wall Street Journal Database; ISI's Science Citation Index on CD-ROM; and Micromedex's Drugdex, Emergindex, Indentindex, and Poisindex. The list could go on and on, as this is the category of products that is emerging most quickly and that changes rapidly. Appendix A includes a current list of such databases; it provides the company and address, contact person, and current products as of August, 1988. Review sources and journals listed in Appendix B can be used to update this list on a regular basis.

Full-Text Databases

Full-text applications have been slower to emerge than have bibliographic or citation-based databases. *Grolier's Electronic Encyclopedia* was the first to be seen at library exhibits. As an early prototype, it was interesting; however, it omitted graphics and illustrations (since corrected). Several examples of reference texts being published in CD-ROM format have emerged during 1987–1988.¹ One example is EBSCO's Serials Directory on CD-ROM, which was demonstrated at the American Library Association 1987 summer conference and which won an ALA award as the best serials publication of 1987. R.R. Bowker is producing a whole series of its reference publications on CD-ROM. The quarterly updated Books-In-Print Plus database consists of 750,000 titles and publisher information on current books in print; it includes *Books in Print, Subject Guide to Books in Print, Books in Print Supplement, Forthcoming Books,* and *Subject Guide to Forthcoming Books.* Ulrich's Plus, a separate Bowker database, consists of 68,000 periodicals listed by title from *Ulrich's International Periodicals Directory,* 36,000 titles from *Irregular Serials and Annuals,* an ISSN index that lists 75,000 current and 13,800 former ISSN titles, and the International Serials Database update. It includes a separate file of complete names and addresses of all publishers.¹ The virtue of the Bowker publications is that they consolidate many Bowker print publications onto one CD-ROM disc which can be searched using keyword and Boolean logic. These databases can also be used to create orders in Bowker's CD-ROM-based acquisitions system.

Complexity of full-text retrieval software, need for efficient retrieval design from CAV-based CD-ROM discs, and the inability to handle graphics efficiently on CD-ROM have slowed the development of full-text products. Emergence of retrieval software such as BlueFish (purchased in 1987 by Lotus); FastFind Plus (used by SAIC in the National Agricultural Text Digitizing Project); Personal Library Software; University Microfilm International's search software; Knowledge Access software; OCLC's announced reference series software; improved scanning techniques for conversion of back files to machine-readable form; development of international standards for typesetting representation; and new compression algorithms for storage and presentation of graphics should result in a number of full text optical publications or demonstration projects during 1988–1989. Several demonstration projects that test full-text applications are underway. Some are described below.

The Library of Congress has had several optical demonstration projects underway since 1983, one on full-text retrieval of periodical literature using digital data discs in a jukebox arrangement; another with sound recordings using a compressed audio disc; a third with graphics and motion pictures on digital videodisc; and a fourth using

CD-ROM for storage and distribution of cataloging information. According to *Optical Disk Circular No. 25,*

> The Optical Disk Serials file, one of five optical disk files, was moved into production status in June [1987] and, pending the preparation of user documentation, will soon be made available to the public. This file links Information Access Corporation's Magazine Index to images of thirty high-use periodical titles for which copyright permission has been granted to scan, store, display, and print. To date, the file contains 71,838 images from full issues of all of 1986 and staff has now scanned about half of the 1985 issues. Issues for 1987 will be scanned as the indexing becomes available. The *Congressional Record* for the 99th Congress is complete and contains 74,340 images; the *Congressional Record* for the 100th Congress is being scanned as it becomes available; the file currently contains over 15,000 images. The BIBL file containing journal articles on public affairs topics now consists of 69,705 images. The contents of all of these files reside on sixty 12" optical disks in a jukebox and are available at five public terminals in the Library's reading rooms.[2]

During the last year of this pilot, efforts are being focused on achieving a consistent rate of input for the present configuration of staff, equipment, and management; monitoring system reliability; and continuing research on the preservation qualities of optical discs.[3]

The National Agricultural Text Digitizing Project (NATDP) is an example of a program which is using CD-ROM and WORM technology to convert and store full-text databases for collection development. Forty-three land-grant libraries have entered into a demonstration project with the National Agricultural Library (NAL) to use scanning and digitizing equipment to convert full-text to machine-readable format and to produce the text on CD-ROM with appropriate search software. The discs will be distributed to the land-grant libraries for national access to these collections, which will include material on subjects such as aquaculture, acid rain, agent orange, food irradiation, and other material of interest to the agricultural community. Systems integration is being provided under contract with Science Applications International Corporation (SAIC), which is using Ricoh scanners to create bit-mapped images of the pages, a Palantir CDP to take the bit-mapped images and convert them via character recognition software to digitized ASCII code, and a WORM drive which records both the bit-mapped image and ASCII code. The data on the WORM drive are indexed, and headers for each page can be keyed in with such information as bibliographic descriptions and key words. The WORM drive is used on the editing station for error correction, after which the data on the WORM drive are recorded on magnetic tape or another WORM disc and sent to the CD-ROM plant for mastering and replication. Search software (FastFind Plus) is being provided on separate floppy disks under a software licensing agreement.[4] Figure 8 shows the process used in this project; Figure 9 shows the actual sequence from scanning through recording onto the WORM drive.

Figure 8: SAIC Image Archive and Full Text Retrieval System

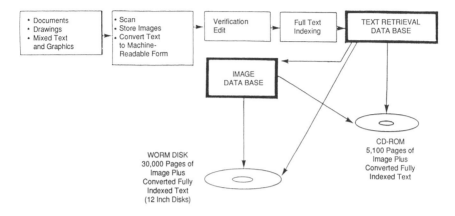

(Reproduced by permission of Science Applications International Corporation, Digital Information Systems Group, McLean, Virginia 22102)

In September 1987, the publishing industry announced that the ADONIS project, a joint effort by ten commercial publishers to distribute full text in electronic format, had been reborn. Participating publishers are Blackwell Scientific Publications, Butterworth Scientific, Churchill Livingstone, Elsevier Science Publishers, C.V. Mosby, Munksgaard International, Pergamon Journals Ltd., Springer-Verlag, Georg Thieme Verlag, and John Wiley & Sons.[5] ADONIS is a trial document-delivery service that supplies biomedical journals published in 1987 and 1988 on CD-ROM. The approximately weekly discs are delivered to twelve major document supply centers in Europe, the U.S.A., Mexico, Australia, and Japan and are used to fulfill requests for individual articles received by the centers.[6]

> The original ADONIS concept was based on the hypothesis that if new technology could be used to fulfill requests more cheaply than the current labour intensive photocopying procedures, the money saved could be shared with copyright holders without substantially changing the price that the centres charged for the supply of documents.[7]

Each week the contents of 218 journals are indexed (according to bibliographic details, not subject indexing) at Excerpta Medica in Amsterdam, the Netherlands. Each item indexed (articles, letters, abstracts, and other material of lasting editorial interest, but not announcements, contents pages, or advertisements) is identified by a unique ADONIS article number. The index information is sent in

Figure 9: NATDP Digitizing and Production Process

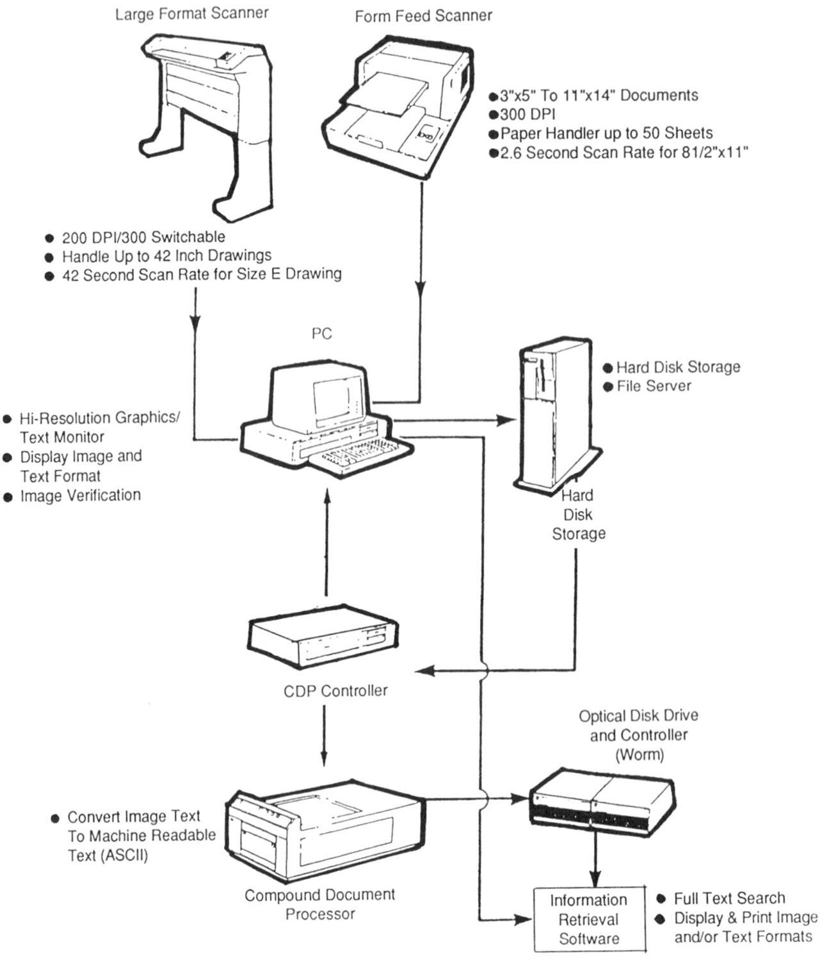

Large Format Scanner

Form Feed Scanner

- 3"x5" To 11"x14" Documents
- 300 DPI
- Paper Handler up to 50 Sheets
- 2.6 Second Scan Rate for 81/2"x11"

- 200 DPI/300 Switchable
- Handle Up to 42 Inch Drawings
- 42 Second Scan Rate for Size E Drawing

PC

- Hard Disk Storage
- File Server

- Hi-Resolution Graphics/
  Text Monitor
- Display Image and
  Text Format
- Image Verification

Hard
Disk
Storage

CDP Controller

Optical Disk Drive
and Controller
(Worm)

- Convert Image Text
  To Machine Readable
  Text (ASCII)

Compound Document
Processor

Information	● Full Text Search
Retrieval	◆ Display & Print Image
Software	and/or Text Formats

(Reproduced by permission of Science Applications International Corporation, Digital
Information Systems Group, McLean, Virginia 22102)

machine-readable form (ASCII) to the Scanmedia bureau in London,
where the contents of the articles are scanned. The scanned contents
together with the ASCII index information are then preformatted,
and a weekly master disc is produced by Philips and DuPont Optical
Company (PDO) in Hannover, West Germany, from which copies are
prepared and dispatched to the participating document output centers. Each disc will carry the index information as well as the digital
representation of the articles. The center can read the index information and store it in a cumulating ADONIS current-awareness index to
match incoming article requests.[8]

The work station design for the ADONIS station is basically that of the LaserData system, using an IBM PC (XT or AT) or compatible computer, an optional high-resolution (300 x 300 pel) monitor capable of displaying a full journal page, proprietary cards (to handle decompression, interface with the disc drive and printer, etc.), a Hitachi CD-ROM drive, and a Ricoh laser printer.[9]

The GraphText project at OCLC is a similar experiment in electronic access to large, full-text reference works. John Wiley and Sons has provided OCLC with machine-readable files and two copies of the *Kirk-Othmer Encyclopedia of Chemical Technology;* the entire 25,000-page encyclopedia, including graphics, equations, tables, and complete indexing, could fit on a single CD-ROM disc. The project involves converting the Wiley files into a standard typesetting format, indexing them, scanning the graphics, adding pointers from the text to the graphics storage location, and developing a user interface for accessing this complex publication.[10] A separate but related project at OCLC is the EIDOS project, which is a prototype search and retrieval system for full text stored in a centralized online database. It is designed to aid the user in moving around the text by such means as windowing and mouse control, as well as providing the ability to take notes.[11]

While there is growing activity in experimentation with full text storage and retrieval, the only actual products, through mid–1988, still fell into the category of bibliographic or indexing products, such as the EBSCO and Bowker publications, or text without graphics, such as the *Grolier Electronic Encyclopedia* and *The Bible Library* (consisting of nine Bibles and 18 reference works). Commercially available full-text-with-graphics applications are beginning to appear, however. *Grolier Electronic Encyclopedia* was released in a new edition with graphics during the summer of 1988, and announced for the first quarter of 1989 is *Facts on File Visual Dictionary CD-ROM,* which will integrate audio, graphics, and text.

Public Access Catalogs

Six companies had announced production of public access catalogs on CD-ROM or digital videodisc by the June 1987 American Library Association conference in San Francisco: Library Corporation, Autographics, General Research Corporation, Marcive, Brodart, and Library Systems & Services, Inc.[12]

CD-ROM catalogs have the advantage of flexible Boolean and key-word searching, as compared to linear searching of microform catalogs. They also have no telecommunications costs or central computer costs, unlike online catalogs. Whether they are more cost-effective than online catalogs will vary according to the size of the library's database, the number of stations, the geographic distances requiring telecommunications, and disc production costs versus computer storage and processing costs. The drawback is, of course, that they are updated much less frequently than an online catalog.

Union Catalogs for Interlibrary Loan

Washington Library Network's LaserCat is an example of a union catalog with member library holdings which can be used to identify owning libraries for interlibrary loan purposes. LaserCat was released by WLN in January 1987 and currently has over 100 systems in the field. The database consists of 1.8 million records held by WLN libraries, plus the most current two years of Library of Congress records.[13] Several state libraries and regional consortia are looking at CD-ROM union catalogs as alternatives to online access between noncompatible systems or to the expense of online access to national utilities such as OCLC.

Bibliographic Instruction

Because databases on CD-ROM or digital videodisc have no connect-time charges, such as online services have, they offer the opportunity for incorporation into bibliographic instruction programs, whereby faculty and students can learn the techniques of Boolean logic without additional cost to the library. The University of Vermont Libraries has taught over 1,000 individuals the concepts of Boolean logic and allows them to use various CD-ROM and online end-user databases without charge; approximately one-third of the reference department's instructional efforts are being geared toward computerized literature searching, using CD-ROM databases and the NOTIS online catalog as instructional tools.[14] Libraries increasingly will be challenged to teach the concepts of database searching in order to help library patrons become as comfortable using electronic forms of information as they have been using traditional print and microform formats. The access to optical databases within the library, without telecommunications costs, provides a cost-effective tool for this instruction.

TECHNICAL SERVICES

Retrospective Conversion

A number of companies have begun to distribute MARC cataloging records from the Library of Congress on CD-ROM. These are being used most heavily by small public libraries for retrospective conversion of cataloging records to machine-readable format. Some state libraries are circulating such systems throughout their state to aid small libraries in retrospective conversion.

Typically, the individual searches the disc, locates the record, and copies it onto floppy disk. The floppy disks are sent to the vendor's central facility, where a master database for the library is built. The advantage to this method over converting records while online with a national utility is the saving in telecommunication charges. The per-record charge also tends to be lower than when a library obtains the records by online conversion or by shipping its shelf list to a central facility like OCLC or AMIGOS Bibliographic Council. Also, the conversion can be done within the library, so that the library staff can interpret local practices in the records.

Companies offering these services are Library Corporation (BiblioFile), with 1,200 installations as of July 1988; General Research Corporation (LaserQuest), with 100 installations as of March 1987; Library Systems & Services, Inc. (Spectrum 400/800 Series); Washington Library Network (LaserCat), and OCLC (now field-testing CD-Cataloging).[15] Faxon is providing a serials database on CD-ROM to aid in conversion of serial titles into its serial order system. Each vendor's database is based on a core of LC-MARC records. Each database also contains other records, varying with the vendor. For instance, General Research Corporation's database includes 260,000 CANMARC records and 2.3 million member-contributed records, in addition to the 2.2 million Library of Congress records. Thus, it is very important when comparing these vendor products to consider the composition of the databases and to predict how good a hit rate one's own library is likely to achieve from a particular database. Large academic libraries, for instance, are likely to find the hit rate much lower using a commercial vendor's database that lacks input from research libraries than when using one of the online national bibliographic utilities such as OCLC, RLIN, or UTLAS, due to the number of esoteric titles which are cataloged by research academic libraries that are members of the online network. By comparison, a small public library may have a hit rate of over 90 percent from a vendor's CD-ROM database, since it probably owns fewer esoteric or little-used titles.

Current Cataloging

The same vendor systems described for retrospective conversion can be used for current cataloging. The Enhanced BiblioFile, for instance, allows for up to eight work stations to be linked to one LC-MARC database, along with a bar-code reader and hard disk drives for storing and editing local records. OCLC envisions that small libraries for which telecommunications charges have become prohibitive will search and extract records from a CD-ROM subset of the online catalog, searching online via dial access only for those records which cannot be found on the CD-ROM portion of the database. The combination of CD-ROM and dial-access online searching would eliminate the cost of the dedicated line to OCLC. The new OCLC telecommunications network is being designed to provide much more dial access capacity for this very reason.

The Library of Congress's "Disc Distribution Pilot Project" demonstrated its first prototype, SDMARC Subjects, in June 1987, to be followed by a two- to three-disc prototype version of the complete LC Name Authority file. Work on a prototype version of the complete USMARC distribution service of all bibliographic records in all formats (books, serials, map, visual materials, and music) also is projected. Test sites were to be equipped with IBMPC/AT's, Hercules Plus and InColor graphics cards, monochrome and color monitors, up to 8 CD-ROM readers per station, and Hewlitt Packard LaserJet Plus printers. The CDMARC Complete is projected to occupy as many as eight drives.[16] SDMARC Subjects was announced as a commercially available product by the Library of Congress Cataloging Distribution Service in the spring of 1988 and was advertised for $300 (U.S.) or $370 (international) in June, 1988,

Acquisitions

At present there are two acquisitions systems using CD-ROM: Ingram's LaserSearch and Bowker's Books-In-Print Plus and Ulrich's Plus. LaserSearch is used in conjunction with Library Corporation's ANYBOOK database, which includes 1.5 million English-language titles in print, or published in the last fifteen years, and is built from tape or catalog data sent from 22,000 publishers. The LaserSearch system allows for searching a title in the ANYBOOK database (in which Ingram titles are highlighted); the ability to provide electronic transmission of orders to Ingram; the ability to print purchase orders to other publishers on three-by-five-inch slips; a check-in system for orders received; and a fund accounting capability of up to 200 funds. The Bowker system allows electronic transmission of purchase orders to Blackwell North America, Brodart, Ingram, and Baker & Taylor. There is an edit screen to create purchase orders for items not in the database. In both cases, there is no interface to local acquisition or in-house systems, although Bowker anticipates adding this feature in the future.[17]

ARCHIVAL APPLICATIONS

At present, most institutions are reluctant to consider optical technology for archival applications. A 1984 white paper prepared by Subcommittee C, Committee on Preservation of the National Archives and Record Service (NARA), recommended that the majority of NARA's holdings continue to be on human-readable microfilm due to the lack of knowledge about shelf life of electronic media and rapid obsolescence in hardware and software.[18] Preservation projects continue to rely on microfilm for this reason. More research into the physical properties of CD-ROM and optical digital discs is needed, and its durability over long periods of time must be demonstrated before optical technology is likely to be used in archival applications, though the Error Detection and Correction (EDAC) methodology espoused by William Nugent offers another approach to this problem. Manufacturers at present will predict no more than a 10- to-30-year shelf life. Thus CD-ROM currently is most applicable to publications which are updated frequently in new editions, such as databases and reference works.

The Library of Congress has begun work on evaluating optical technology for preservation purposes. William Nugent has written about the use of Error Detection and Correction (EDAC) methods as an approach to using optical technology for preservation:

> While it would be cost-effective to have optical recording media last several hundred years, such media do not exist today, nor are they needed for purposes of preserving digital information. The information encoded on an optical disk can be made to survive indefinitely by rewriting the digital information onto a new disk. Flawless duplication can be ensured by means of powerful Error Detection and Correction (EDAC) systems.[19]

The American National Standards Institute X3B11 Ad Hoc Subcommittee on EDAC for optical systems is chaired by Nugent. The subcommittee has been considering proposals for EDAC systems based on considerations of disc overhead space, complexity, execution time, and performance. Its objectives include obtaining agreement on three items: specifications for minimum "start-of-life" media quality, specifications for "end-of-life" quality, and a model of defect distribution on the disk at end-of-life. Alternate proposals for accomplishing those objectives are to be evaluated. This approach views discs as an "information" preservation medium with an orderly process of periodic inspection and replication of discs as needed.[20]

SOFTWARE TRANSPORTABILITY

One nonpublishing application for CD-ROM is its ability to store computer programs for wide distribution. One vendor which has taken advantage of this ability is PC-SIG, which is distributing all of its software on a CD-ROM for $295 (as of August 1988); all of those programs can be downloaded into a microcomputer. Reference Technology Inc. is advertising its *Software Library DataPlate* on CD-ROM for $195; the largest publisher in this class is Alde Publishing Company with six public-domain CD-ROMS, including *Software du Jour,* containing 365 shareware programs for $29.95. CD-ROM is preferable to floppy disks or magnetic tape for transport of large programs or many small programs to many users because of its durability and the access to CD-ROM drives by microcomputer users, as compared to magnetic tape drives. It also allows direct downloading into the microcomputer. This application will become more common as the number of CD-ROM drives in use by libraries and microcomputer users increases.

AUDIOVISUAL APPLICATIONS

Digital videodisc, CDI, and DVI will be most applicable to audiovisual uses and educational learning packages which require interactive software with graphics capability. Compression techniques will improve the storage capacity for graphics on CD-ROM, which will be useful for publications which include photographs, maps, charts or tables. The requirements for interactive software with motion and graphics capabilities or for extensive high-resolution color photographs or motion will most likely continue to outstrip the technical capabilities of CD-ROM, WORM, or ODD. Thus, the most likely future markets for CDI, DVI, or digital videodisc will be in educational software; in the segment of the publishing market which requires high-resolution graphics or extensive color photographs; and in the preservation of photographs, motion pictures, and sound recordings. It is this last archival need which is the focus of the Library of Congress's nonprint optical pilot projects, which use analog videodisc technology to preserve and make available paper prints of motion pictures, selections from the library's vast pictorial collections, and a 33-hour compressed audio disk of 668 early sound recordings, including nearly every spoken-word disk manufactured before 1910 in the library's collections, 55 Nation's Forum discs, and recordings of prominent American political figures.[21]

OFFICE APPLICATIONS

The most promising optical medium for office applications is WORM technology. Office applications usually need only one "file" copy for in-house reports, correspondence, accounting information, and the like. Much of this material need be held for only short periods of time. For instance, historical accounting files can usually be discarded after five to seven years. The WORM technology allows copies of these files to be made directly from word-processing, spreadsheet, or other microcomputer systems; to be searched by flexible retrieval software; and to be much more compact than file cabinets. Where institutional material needs to be saved for extended periods of time, WORM technology is probably not a good option at present, given the lack of knowledge about its long-term shelf life. Given the amount of information which can be stored on a WORM disc, some indexing scheme to know what is on each disc should be employed.

COMPUTING CENTERS

Computing centers are looking to optical digital data discs for the storage of very large databases that require multiple-user access over a network. If the discs are housed in a jukebox arrangement, physical retrieval of the discs by mechanical means is possible, thus mechanizing retrieval of the data. Eliminating human intervention in the data access methodology is very important for network access that might have a high volume of activity and that will require multiple discs for storage of large databases. Cornell University Libraries has indicated to the National Agricultural Library that it is seeking grant funds to explore this application for large library data files.[22]

The system used in one of the Library of Congress pilot projects already employs this technology (see Figure 10 for an illustration of the relationships between the IBM computer system, the Data General computer system, and the video system controller). In the LC configuration, devices such as scanners, storage systems, juke boxes, high-speed printers, and terminal controllers connect to a Video System Controller (VSC) which controls the image storage and retrieval. The VSC is controlled from two sources: a Data General minicomputer for document input, and an IBM 3084 mainframe for image retrieval. Both machines send instructions to the VSC through communications ports, directing the transfer of image data from one device to another. The image does not go through either the IBM or the Data General. The image terminals are VT100-compatible high-resolution monitors interfacing directly to the IBM for alphanumeric communications and to the VSC for images. The interface is necessary so that the indexing for the scanned data, which already exists in

Figure 10: LC Document Storage and Retrieval System

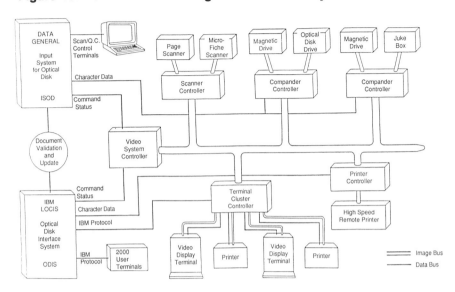

(Reproduced by permission of Basil Manns, The Library of Congress)

the public SCORPIO indexing system, can be used to identify material and then interface with the optical disc system for text and image retrieval.[23] The jukebox used was developed under contract by Integrated Automation.[24]

REFERENCES

1. Campbell, Brian. "Whither the White Knight: CD-ROM in Technical Services." *DATABASE* 10 (4) (August 1987): 27.

2. Library of Congress. Optical Disk Pilot Program. *Optical Disk Circular No. 25* (August 1987): 2.

3. *Optical Disk Circular No. 25, 2.*

4. University of Vermont and State Agricultural College. Contract with Science Applications International Corporation, under the Cooperative Agreement between the University of Vermont and the National Agricultural Library for the National Agricultural Text Digitizing Project. 1987.

5. Campbell, Robert M., and Stern, Barrie T. "ADONIS—A New Approach to Document Delivery." *Microcomputers for Information Management* 4 (2) (June 1987): 95.

6. *ADONIS: The Facts.* (brochure) Available from the ADONIS Project Director, P.O. Box 2400, 1000CK Amsterdam, the Netherlands. (A/3P076/10.000/0786)

7. *ADONIS: The Facts.*

8. Campbell and Stern, 95.

9. Campbell and Stern, 96.

10. *OCLC Newsletter* 169 (July/August 1987): 16.

11. Demonstration at OCLC for Nancy L. Eaton, September 23, 1987.

12. Campbell, 28–40.

13. Campbell, 26.

14. See University of Vermont Case Study, chapter 9.

15. Campbell, 28–40.

16. Library of Congress. National Bibliographic Services. *CDS Product News: CDMARC Subjects* (June 1987).

17. Campbell, 27, 32–35.

18. Mallinson, John C. "On the Preservation of Human- and Machine-Readable Records." *Information Technology and Libraries* 7 (1) (March 1988): 19–23.

19. Library of Congress. National Preservation News [No. 4] (April 1986): 11.

20. *National Preservation News,* 12.

21. *Optical Disk Circular No. 25:* 1.

22. Letter from Cornell University to National Agricultural Library, 1987.

23. Manns, Basil, and Wilder, Dean. "Interfacing a Mainframe Database Retrieval System with an Optical Disk Image Storage System." Presentation at the IEEE Mass Storage Symposium in Tucson, Arizona (May 1987): 1.

24. Manns, Basil, and Swora, Tamara. "ITS: Digital Imaging at the Library of Congress." *Journal of Information and Image Management* (October 1986): 28–29.

Chapter 3
Software Design and Retrieval Issues

The vital function of CD-ROM software in a library is communication: Software makes it possible to select, examine, arrange, and produce information from the optical storage medium. This chapter is intended to help a librarian understand how the software in an optical system operates and to provide guidelines for evaluating software on the basis of how well it performs these tasks.

While many articles and promotional releases about CD-ROM technology paint glowing pictures of the medium's storage capabilities, optical discs pose special problems in information retrieval for software developers. Stated simply, you can get a lot of information *on* an optical disc, but it's not easy to design efficient programs that get *back* just the information you want. The major problems in retrieval involve the very large numbers of very large files on the disc and the way the reading mechanism has to move to find the sectors where the information is located. These issues are discussed in detail in several of the articles cited in the bibliography (Appendix B).

STANDARDS IN SOFTWARE DEVELOPMENT

The role of standards in software development, as discussed in chapter 1, is very important in considering retrieval issues. Central to the discussion of software standards is the concept of the disc's logical format. Logical format, according to software designer Bill Zoellick, "determines such matters as where to place fundamental identifying information on the disc, where to find the directory of the files on the disc, how the directory is structured, and so on. It should not be confused with the actual physical format of the disc, which determines whether the disc will work with a specific player."[1] Unlike the physical format of the disc, the logical format has not been formally standardized, although a voluntary group of hardware and software companies known as the High Sierra Group has proposed a minimum set of logical standards to the National Information Standards Organization (NISO). Standardization in logical formats is as important as the physical recording standards now in practice. The hardware standards are intended to ensure that any CD-ROM disc can be read in any drive; however, the lack of logical, or data, standards means that a disc prepared by one company may not be able to be read by the software of another vendor. For example, if a work station is running SilverPlatter's ERIC disc, the user cannot open the disc drive, replace the ERIC disc with the WILSONDISC Education Index, and continue working. Instead, the user must also change to Wilson's software. Librarians planning work station requirements for optical products have to allow for software and disc changes when users want to switch databases, or else provide expensive "dedicated" work stations for each product.

The logical format may be thought of as a group of rules or definitions governing how certain information is structured and where it is located on the disc. Origination software assembles files for the CD-ROM disc according to the rules of the logical format; this is a writing function and is part of the production process. Librarians will usually be most involved with retrieval software, for these are the programs that provide access to or read the files on the disc. Retrieval software is part of the user interface, which also includes the display screens, keyboard commands, and searching and processing (printing, downloading, editing) functions of the optical system. Unlike the logical format, standardization of retrieval software is unlikely to happen at this early stage of optical product development, nor would it necessarily be the best thing. Information providers are trying to develop distinctive products; to foster "brand loyalty," the user interface must be significantly different from that of other products in the field. Vendors are also committed to being as up-to-date as possible in this new medium. It is to the librarian's advantage to have a variety of approaches to choose from and to test and compare the new offerings with a view toward how well they do the tasks at hand.

MODES OF INFORMATION RETRIEVAL

Information consultant Nancy Herther observes that "whether used for individualized archival/database management systems, bibliographic retrieval, or full-text information storage, the information contained on a disk has value only if it is easily accessible. This requires that the software be designed so that it is not only user-friendly but also effective in retrieving information...."[2] Although optical disc technology is still very new, a wide range of search capabilities is available (see Figure 11).

Figure 11: Retrieval Modes

RETRIEVAL MODE	FULL TEXT	BIBLIOGRAPHIC	LIBRARY
Paper-Based: browse index or keyword	InfoTrac's *Wall St. Journal*	InfoTrac Newsbank	LaserQuest LaserSearch
Online: Multi-term or implicit Boolean	*CFR /* *Federal Register* Microsoft Bookshelf	Books in Print Plus Dissertation Abstracts	Bibliofile Le Pac LaserGuide
Online: full Boolean		SilverPlatter OCLC Search CD450	
Paper/Online combinations	Grolier Electronic Encyclopedia	Compact Cambridge Compact Disclosure	
Optical/Online combinations	DaText	Wilsondisc DialogOnDisc	

Paper-Based Interfaces

Some products closely reflect the information-management tools with which *both* librarians and users are most familiar: print sources. Paper has certain physical limitations as an information medium. It is often called a "linear" medium because reading is done line by line and page by page. There are severe limits on the amount of type that can fit on one page, and lots of page turning is necessary to find information located in other sections or volumes. Outlines, indexes, footnotes, "see" references, tables of contents, and bibliographies are some of the methods that have been developed to cope with paper's limitations. InfoTrac and Newsbank are optical products whose search capabilities correspond to those of paper sources: The search process leads to a subject heading with references listed under it. The optical enhancements are limited to speeding up the functions of checking the controlled subject headings, moving from one subject heading to another ("page turning"), and printing the search results. Because of the way they present information, these products are the most likely to seem familiar to the new user. However, they are very elementary applications of optical technology.

Online Interfaces

Some optical products' search programs seem to be derived from methods of online searching, which is another tool that has grown familiar to many librarians. The subject-heading search mechanisms mentioned above provide manageable results only because the database is restricted to recent citations. Therefore, each subject heading can usually be expected to yield a number of citations that can be viewed on a few screens. But the storage capabilities of optical technology, one of its strongest selling points, make it possible to offer databases that contain twenty years of *Psychological Abstracts* or millions of MARC records. Such large databases demand the use of Boolean operators, truncation, field qualification, nested logic, and other refinements that are routinely used in online searching.

Some optical products simplify the search process by using screen displays that include special lines or boxes where search terms are entered; the terms are then joined by "implicit logic" in which the software inserts a predetermined Boolean operator (usually AND) and may also add truncation and nesting parentheses as required. Books-In-Print Plus, LaserGuide, and Microsoft's Bookshelf are examples of products that handle searching in this way. SilverPlatter search software, on the other hand, offers full Boolean operators, truncation, nested logic, and field qualification by commands that are included in the search statement just as they are in online searching.

Paper/Online Combinations

Some optical disc products combine elements of both print and online. WILSONDISC has four separate retrieval modes: "Browse" to search the index by subject heading; "Wilsearch" to use a work form with implicit logic; "Wilsonline" to use commands for Boolean operators and nesting; and "Expert" to utilize advanced options. Grolier's Electronic Encyclopedia has a "Browse" search method to use index subject headings to locate the main article on a topic and a "Word Search" method to search for terms through the full text of the encyclopedia. DIALOG OnDisc, Datext, and Compact Disclosure are other products that combine one or more retrieval methods.

Optical/Online Combinations

Datext, DIALOG OnDisc, and WILSONDISC are also among the first products to combine access to *both* optical and online databases at the same work station. The long lead time required to assemble, master, and produce optical discs makes a quarterly schedule the most frequent updating that is practical. Users who require more recent materials can search the extensive backfiles stored on optical disc, then dial out to check the updated materials online. Currently being developed is intelligent software that will recognize when a query should be automatically routed to the updated files.

Hierarchies and Hypertext

Advanced as the retrieval combinations above may sound, even more sophisticated retrieval methods are underway, methods that take advantage of optical disc technology's special characteristics. All of the print and online methods are superimposed on optical discs to make them look like more familiar information-management tools such as paper indexes or online search system interfaces. Optical disc technology linked to microcomputers can manipulate and present information in ways that have only begun to be explored by the most forward-thinking software designers. Robert Carr, director of technology at Ashton-Tate, states that "It is not enough for electronic publishing to lay information down on the CD ROM in the identical format used in print publishing; it's not even enough to have a 'sugar coating' of fast keyword searching added over the raw data. Users need multiple access paths to the information."[3] Carr calls these paths "hierarchies" or electronic outlines, which allow the searcher to move from one topic to related topics at various levels of detail. He gives an example of a user researching *metals* down to *alloys*, then following *alloys* to *bioengineering* and learning that some alloys are used as bone replacements.

Moving from topic to topic and among varying levels of information would quickly become confusing, but the microcomputer is capable of keeping track of the path or hierarchy the user has followed. To use a familiar print example, the searcher would write outlines, notes, and comments on the microcomputer's hard disk to store the research path much as we now use highlighting, underlining, and note cards to manage references. Other writers call this approach to retrieval "hypertext." Tim Oren and Gary Kildall describe hypertext as a system that "provides direct links to cited articles at the point of reference and, through a full indexing system, it can show all the citations of a document under study. With this capability, the researcher can move quickly through networks of related information, saving the browse path as a personalized index."[4] T.J. Byers states that hypertext "approaches data storage and retrieval associatively; a body of information is referenced within itself rather than to an outside directory. The ideal hypertext environment would solve the storage-and-retrieval problem by using a three-dimensional network of logical data links modeled after human intelligence."[5] Byers also describes an application of hypertext: the KnowledgeSet version of Grolier's Electronic Encyclopedia, which features linked references, a path that "remembers" where the user has searched, and indexing of related encyclopedia entries. Byers calls this version an example of "static" hypertext, since the links were added by the producer and cannot be changed or enhanced by the user. Static is differentiated from "dynamic" hypertext, which would allow the user to create new links and add new documents to the database. Dynamic hypertext is very similar to the system Carr envisions, but Byers feels that the technology used will be WORM (write-once, read-many) drives instead of CD-Roms with magnetic disks. Owl International's Guide and The Box Company's Window Book are examples of hypertext software currently available for IBM PC and Apple Macintosh computers, with CD-ROM applications in development.

Byers also describes a medium which combines hypertext, graphics, and audio databases into a new optical product: "hypermedia." A hypermedia document about Johann Sebastian Bach which referred to a certain musical passage would "display the text, play the piece, and call up a slide show to entertain you during the performance."[6] Recent developments in software for both IBM and Apple computers have made hypermedia available for magnetic disk applications, and optical disc versions are forecast within one year. Apple's HyperCard combines searching, programming, and graphics functions with audio capabilities, using an icon-based approach that makes it easier for non-programmers to assemble and publish data. A version of *The Whole Earth Catalog* called The Whole Earth Learning Disk is currently being developed using HyperCard for release on CD-ROM. The Intermedia Project at Brown University is a hypermedia system based on UNIX software that allows users to create webs of links between text and graphics documents; it has been successfully used for English and biology college courses.

USER INTERFACES

For most librarians investigating optical disc products, the user interface will be the most important software factor to consider and evaluate. The user interface, according to David Miller of DCM Associates, "consists of the microcomputer screen displays and keyboard commands provided to CD-ROM users. It is through the user interface that the user learns what is on a disk, finds and retrieves desired information, and manages whatever is done to process the information thereafter."[7] The user interface includes the retrieval modes, post-processing options, documentation, and vendor support that characterize the product. Evaluating user interfaces is an important task for the librarian considering the purchase of optical disc products; the following discussion will offer guidelines for evaluation of various interface functions. Because most of the products currently available to libraries are in the CD-ROM or videodisc (read-only) formats, the information will apply to these formats.

Screen Displays

Screen displays are the first thing the user sees and must be assessed with reference to the intended users of the product. For end users, the first screen displays should identify the product and give essential information such as the time segment of the database contained on the disc currently in the drive. SilverPlatter's introductory screens are good examples; they provide the name of the database, years covered on the disc, a paragraph-long description of the content of the database, and commands for further information about the database and the system. The current function is in capital letters at the bottom of the screen, so the user knows what the system is ready to do. There are also easy-to-follow prompts to call up the help screens if necessary (see Figure 12).

Figure 12: SilverPlatter/ERIC Title Screen

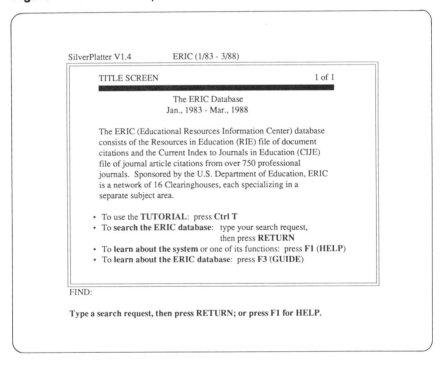

SilverPlatter V1.4   ERIC (1/83 - 3/88)

TITLE SCREEN   1 of 1

The ERIC Database
Jan., 1983 - Mar., 1988

The ERIC (Educational Resources Information Center) database
consists of the Resources in Education (RIE) file of document
citations and the Current Index to Journals in Education (CIJE)
file of journal article citations from over 750 professional
journals. Sponsored by the U.S. Department of Education, ERIC
is a network of 16 Clearinghouses, each specializing in a
separate subject area.

• To use the **TUTORIAL**: press **Ctrl T**
• To **search the ERIC database**: type your search request,
                                    then press **RETURN**
• To **learn about the system** or one of its functions: press **F1 (HELP)**
• To **learn about the ERIC database**: press **F3 (GUIDE)**

FIND:

Type a search request, then press RETURN; or press F1 for HELP.

(Reprinted with permission from SilverPlatter Information, Inc. Copyright © 1988)

Screens should be clearly organized, but not necessarily along the lines of print resources. Many optical products are making innovative use of the screen's graphic capabilities, such as windowing, scrolling, painting, and color. Librarians who are not familiar with these displays must be careful not to reject them without using the product long enough to be sure that it is the organization of information that is confusing rather than the method of presentation. Present-day library users, especially younger ones, are very familiar with video effects and will usually be very receptive to these lively displays.

Screen displays for products like Bibliofile and Books-In-Print Plus, which are more likely to be used by library staff, should be evaluated on the basis that their users can be trained and will probably be using the system frequently. These products need not provide the constant elementary prompts and reminders that are required for end-user systems.

Retrieval Modes

The search capabilities of the product should also correspond to its purpose. Most vendors have carefully designed their search options to meet the needs of certain groups of users, such as new searchers, technical services librarians, or physicians. The usual functions are Boolean operators, truncation, term expansion, field qualification, and nested logic, but they are handled in a seemingly infinite variety of ways. For example, no two systems to date use the same symbol for truncation. The librarian who is very familiar with one or more established online search services may be at a disadvantage in evaluating these highly individual products and must be open to exploring new ways of handling the standard search functions. SilverPlatter, for example, handles field qualification by adding the word "in" with a two-letter field label: **anxiety in ti**. This approach might seem cumbersome to searchers who are accustomed to using punctuation marks for the purpose, but is very easy for new users to learn. OCLC's Search CD450 provides field qualification with a colon followed by a two-letter field label: **evolution:ti**. The Wilsearch level on WILSONDISC displays a work form with a special entry line marked **title words**.

Boolean operators may be offered as straightforward commands or as implied functions in multiterm or menu-driven systems. The command-driven products should give a list of commands and the ways they function. In addition to AND, OR, and NOT, some products provide one or more positional operators, like ADJ, WITH and NEAR. In systems which will accept multiple word entries, there will be a default operator that is important to identify. Searchers will receive different results from the entry **television advertisements** when the default operator is ADJ than they will get with the default operator AND. Implicit logic systems, in which the operator is inserted automatically when the terms are typed in particular boxes or lines, should indicate clearly how the query will be processed. In

CD/CorpTech, for example, the "screening" search mode has both OR and AND as implicit logical operators; choosing criteria within one category (Boston and Denver within the category "City") will join the terms with OR; selecting two or more categories ("City" and "End Market"), however, combines the categories with AND.

Products that offer a variety of search levels, for both novices and experts, may be more flexible than those that only offer one. New users can start with the easy or browse mode, which is usually a search by subject heading or index keyword (as in Dialog OnDisc), or in a menu-driven mode like Wilsearch, and progress to more complex, command-driven searches. The assisted level builds confidence, and the advanced level frees the experienced searcher from the necessity of stepping through menus that quickly become tiresome. If one of the purposes of the optical product is to provide training or practice time for end users of online services, a command level of sufficient complexity to make exercises meaningful should be available. Whatever options are offered, the search capabilities should be clearly explained. Commands should be concise, with a minimum of key strokes required. Some products offer the ability to save and re-execute search strategies, an important consideration when searching a large database like ERIC that has to be published on several discs. The process of changing and refining a strategy should also be simple. For example, SilverPlatter's software refers to existing sets by number: **#1 and anxiety.** OCLC's Search CD450 uses a function key to call up sets for the addition of more terms or other qualifications. Search result statistics should be clearly indicated and easy to understand (see Figure 13).

Response Time

The tradeoff for the optical disc's ability to store large amounts of data is the disc drive's slow speed of access to that data. Software designers Tim Oren and Gary Kildall describe the technical problems: "The laser pickup head typically requires 0.5 seconds to access information on the innermost tracks, and 1.5 seconds to reach the outer tracks. By contrast, hard-disk units can access data in tens of milliseconds. The CD-ROM is slowed by the mass of its pickup head, which contains a focusing system with several lenses and which must be positioned with extreme accuracy...The slow access rate is a severe drawback for the most common forms of information stored on CD-ROMs: sequential data files, conventional databases, and textual information bases."[8] Slow access time is a relative judgment. Librarians who are used to the power and speed of the major online services will have high standards. New searchers accustomed to paging through indexes, abstracts, and encyclopedias may judge optical disc retrieval speed to be

Figure 13: OCLC Search CD450 Screen with Numeric Counts

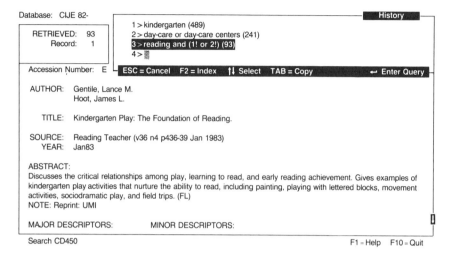

History Window

Database: CIJE 82-

RETRIEVED: 93
Record: 1

| History |
| 1 > kindergarten (489) |
| 2 > day-care or day-care centers (241) |
| 3 > reading and (1! or 2!) (93) |
| 4 > |

Accession Number: E — ESC = Cancel   F2 = Index   ↑↓ Select   TAB = Copy   ↵ Enter Query

AUTHOR: Gentile, Lance M.
          Hoot, James L.

TITLE: Kindergarten Play: The Foundation of Reading.

SOURCE: Reading Teacher (v36 n4 p436-39 Jan 1983)
YEAR: Jan83

ABSTRACT:
Discusses the critical relationships among play, learning to read, and early reading achievement. Gives examples of kindergarten play activities that nurture the ability to read, including painting, playing with lettered blocks, movement activities, sociodramatic play, and field trips. (FL)
NOTE: Reprint: UMI

MAJOR DESCRIPTORS: MINOR DESCRIPTORS:

Search CD450   F1 = Help   F10 = Quit

delightfully quick. Software developers are working to improve speed of retrieval. For product evaluations, test searches should be done at all levels of complexity available on the system. Most products can handle a simple subject heading or keyword search acceptably; processing time may increase, however, as search strategies become more complex, especially when truncation and nested logic are used. If a system offers Boolean operators and nested logic, complex test searches will reveal how access speed is affected. Well-designed display screens also keep the searcher oriented by showing how the search processing is proceeding; one method is to show the percent of records that have been reviewed. The user should be able to break into an ongoing search easily if the processing time continues beyond a reasonable limit.

Post-Processing Capabilities

Post-processing capabilities include the display, print, download, reformat, and edit functions of the software. Some products have very simple options. InfoTrac, for example, displays citations on the screen and scrolls the display up and down by line or by screen; designated function keys print a single reference or a single screen.

Most systems, however, now offer more complex choices. Search results may be provided as screen displays, printed copy, or files to be transferred to diskette. OCLC Search CD450 users can select one of several formats for viewing records, choose record numbers from the display, and have the results printed or saved to hard disk or diskette. In LaserQuest, records can be used to generate catalog card sets and the output can be sorted; the company is developing an option for spine label printing. Products that save records to disk as ASCII files will be useful to users who are interested in editing the results with a word processing program. Other users will want to transfer data into spreadsheet or database management programs. Datext has a particularly sophisticated range of post-processing options: printing a complete or edited version of a document; transferring search results into one of seven software packages, including Lotus 1-2-3, Symphony and WordStar; and downloading in ASCII format to a floppy disk.

Most products use combinations of function keys and screen menus to enable users to select post-processing options. These instructions should be clear and straightforward. In addition to printed templates and search reference cards, an on-screen menu bar listing function keys and their purposes may be helpful. OCLC Search CD450 and WILSONDISC use menu bars effectively (see Figure 14). In bibliographic databases, the default record format must include all of the information necessary to locate the document. Some products, including SilverPlatter and OCLC Search CD450, allow librarians to edit the default format as part of the software setup process.

On-Screen Help

Effective on-screen help is a very important part of the user interface. The optical disc system is built around the capabilities of the microcomputer, and searchers quickly become accustomed to using the keyboard to call up all of the system's functions. Searchers should not have to turn to printed manuals when they need explanations or assistance. Brief keyboard templates or single-page laminated cards placed near the work station are the most extensive printed references that many searchers are willing to consult. System manuals are important primarily for staff reference and problem solving but will not be used by most searchers.

Optical disc user interfaces are fluid structures, as opposed to print materials. Screens may display several windows, and new windows may appear in response to searcher commands. Depending on the complexity of the product, some menus will appear as subsets of other menus or will only be available from a particular command level. In WILSONDISC, some keys have different functions depending on which retrieval mode has been selected. On-screen help must

Figure 14: WILSONDISC Screen with User Option Bar

CITATION DISPLAYED

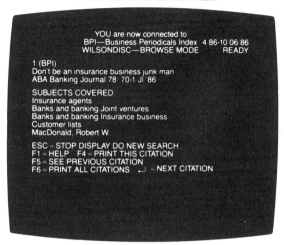

```
        YOU are now connected to
  BPI—Business Periodicals Index  4 86-10 06 86
  WILSONDISC—BROWSE MODE        READY

1 (BPI)
Don't be an insurance business junk man
ABA Banking Journal 78  70-1 Jl  86

SUBJECTS COVERED
Insurance agents
Banks and banking Joint ventures
Banks and banking Insurance business
Customer lists
MacDonald, Robert W.

ESC = STOP DISPLAY DO NEW SEARCH
F1 = HELP   F4 = PRINT THIS CITATION
F5 = SEE PREVIOUS CITATION
F6 = PRINT ALL CITATIONS   ↵ = NEXT CITATION
```

(This is a sample from the Browse mode of H.W. Wilson Company's WILSONDISC CD-ROM retrieval system. Reproduced by permission of H.W. Wilson Company.)

be readily available at any point to keep searchers oriented within the system.

The OCLC Search CD450 and WILSONDISC menu bars mentioned above are examples of good planning for on-screen help. The menu bars list function keys and their purposes; different menu bars appear in response to changes in the search process. An informal convention seems to ensure that when function keys are used, **F1** is designated as the key to call up help screens from any point in the search process. The help screens themselves should be clear and concise, leaving detailed explanations to the printed user's manuals. Good help screens make effective use of highlighting and windowing, and provide instructions for returning to the search process directly.

Documentation

In addition to on-screen help, product vendors should supply adequate documentation to assist librarians in setting up, installing, and using the system. This documentation may include loose-leaf or spiral-bound manuals, keyboard templates, brief reference guides to display near the workstation and similar materials. The documentation should be well organized, very clearly written, and appropriately illustrated. Since optical disc products are so new and improvements to the software are constantly being issued, a polished format is less important than timeliness. A loose-leaf binder may be useful to organize the letters and bulletins that accompany system upgrades, because in many cases the system will be more advanced than the current documentation indicates. Some optical products require two types of documentation: system and database. SilverPlatter documents the software for its versions of ERIC, PsycLIT, and Agricola, but thesauri and user aids for these databases come from the Educational Resources Information Center, the American Psychological Association, and the National Agricultural Library. NewsBank and most of the WILSONDISC indexes are products in which both the system and the database are produced by the same company, although WILSONDISC has recently started to offer other producers' databases, including the Modern Language Association International Bibliography and Film Literature Index. There is no particular advantage to having both system and database come from one vendor; librarians can acquire appropriate documentation from both sources.

If two companies are involved in production, it is essential for the purchaser to understand clearly the responsibilities each is going to assume. Sample points of clarification might include who will determine the update frequency and what it will be; whether one company will handle all of the paperwork or separate contracts and payments must be made; whether the companies have joint products planned for the future; and who will provide what services if the product is discontinued. SilverPlatter and the American Psychological Association, for example, work together to produce PsycLIT. The APA takes responsibility for processing and invoicing orders for the database; SilverPlatter ships the discs, maintains and updates the software, and provides product support and development. Both companies actively market PsycLIT.

Toll-free telephone help is another important form of assistance offered by many companies. Optical disc technology is durable but complex; it is essential to have access to experienced, responsive customer support staff to consult with problems. Some companies have developed reputations for being quick to implement software changes based on customers' recommendations and have formed user groups for more organized interaction and feedback.

SOFTWARE AND RETRIEVAL ISSUES CHECKLIST

Several checklists have been published to assist with optical product evaluation: "A Planning Model for Optical Product Evaluation" by Nancy Herther,[9] "Evaluating CDROMS: To Buy or What to Buy?" by David Miller,[10] and "Picking CD-ROMS for Public Use" by Linda Stewart.[11]

The following checklist outlines criteria for assessing software and retrieval capabilities; its organization is based on the content of chapter 3.

I. User Interface
  A. What impression does the overall interface make?
  B. Is the interface designed for one or more user levels (novice/expert)? Is it menu-driven, command-driven, or a combination?
  C. Are function keys used clearly and appropriately?
II. Screen Displays
  A. Are screen displays clear and well organized?
  B. Do they make effective use of color, graphics, windowing, special features?
  C. Is the display information appropriate for the intended audience?
III. Retrieval Modes
  A. What search features are offered?
    1. Boolean operators? Which ones? Is logic implicit, by command, or a combination?
    2. Positional operators?
    3. Nested logic?
    4. Field qualification? How is it specified?
    5. Wild-card symbols and truncation? Number of characters specified or open?
  B. Can search strategies be modified easily?
  C. Are search statistics clearly displayed?
  D. Can search strategies be saved and re-executed?
  E. Does the system have an online thesaurus? Is it quickly and easily available? What are the protocols for entering controlled language terms?
IV. Response Time
  A. How does the response time compare to that of other media? With that of other optical systems?
  B. Are appropriate processing messages displayed?
  C. Is there a break function?
V. Post-Processing Capabilities
  A. Displaying? Can formats be selected, altered?
  B. Printing? Can citations be viewed first? Can formats be selected, changed? Do default formats include all important information?
  C. Downloading? Can text be saved to disk or diskette? Can files be reformatted, edited, sorted? Are results compatible with popular software programs?
  D. Can default settings for format be changed? Can limits be

placed on number of citations that can be printed or downloaded?
VI. On-Screen Help
  A. Are help screens readily available from any point in search?
  B. Is the information presented on the help screens clear, concise, and effective?
VII. Documentation
  A. What documentation is supplied with the system? User manuals, reference cards, templates, posters?
  B. Are the materials clear, well-illustrated, up-to-date with system capabilities?
  C. If more than one company is involved, what are the responsibilities of each?
  D. Is toll-free telephone assistance provided? During what hours?

REFERENCES

1. Zoellick, Bill. "File System Support for CD ROM." *CD-ROM, The New Papyrus*, edited by Steve Lambert and Suzanne Ropiquet. Bellevue, WA: Microsoft Press, 1986, p. 104.

2. Herther, Nancy. "Access Software for Optical/Laser Information Packages." *DATABASE* 9 (4) (August 1986): 93.

3. Carr, Robert. "New User Interfaces for CD ROM." *CD ROM, The New Papyrus*, edited by Steve Lambert and Suzanne Ropiquet. Bellevue, WA: Microsoft Press, p. 190.

4. Oren, Tim, and Kildall, Gary. "The Compact Disk ROM: Applications Software." *IEEE Spectrum* 23 (4) (April 1986): 54.

5. Byers, T.J. "Built by Association." *PC World* 5 (4) (April 1987): 245.

6. Byers, p. 250.

7. Miller, David C. "Evaluating CDROMS: To Buy or What to Buy?" *DATABASE* 10 (3) (June 1987): 39.

8. Oren and Kildall, p. 50.

9. Herther, p. 93–94.

10. Miller, p. 41–42.

11. Stewart, Linda. "Picking CD-ROMS for Public Use." *American Libraries* 18 (9) (October 1987): 738–740.

Chapter 4
Public Service Considerations

Once a library has made the decision to include optical media in its collection, the library staff in charge of offering optical systems to users may well ask, "Now that we've got it, what do we do with it?" At first glance, optical media may seem a little mysterious and completely different from the print and online media with which librarians are used to dealing. The high cost of each optical disc alone may make librarians hesitant to offer optical databases directly to patrons. Once the microcomputer and disc player have been unpacked, however, and the optical disc itself has been held up and roundly examined, the next step is for librarians to face the details of how optical systems will be offered to users and what service considerations will need to be resolved for the optical disc searcher.

THE PRINT-DISC-ONLINE CONTINUUM

Any new information technology, especially one that promises to revolutionize the way we view information storage and retrieval, must initially be considered in terms of media with which we are already familiar. To see how optically based information sources can fit in with print and online services, it is valuable to compare the characteristics of print and online media to those of optical discs (see Figure 15). The similarities and differences between the three media dictate choices in many service considerations facing libraries as they implement optical technologies.

Cost

Because reference sources on optical disc are generally acquired by annual subscription rather than through timed charges, they have some similarities with their print counterparts. As with print sources, the costs for optical discs are fixed and predictable; both can be searched without regard to time spent in finding individual citations

Figure 15: Print-Disc-Online Continuum

	PRINT	DISC	ONLINE
COST	Fixed Predictable	Fixed Predictable	Variable Unpredictable
CURRENCY	Annual to Semi-monthly Longest Backfile	Quarterly Limited Backfile	Quarterly to Continuously Long Backfile
SEARCH MECHANISMS	Linear Index Terms Linear Display	Many & Varied Search Options Varied Display	Menu-driven or Command-driven Linear Display
AUDIENCE	Librarians to All End-users	Librarians to Some End-users	Librarians to Trained End-users
NUMBER OF USERS	Several, using different volumes	One at a time	Several, depending on the number of passwords
USE	Begin Search Simple Search	Refine Search Multi-concept Search	Update/Retrospective Search Complex Searches

and abstracts. This one simple similarity has a powerful impact on how use protocols and training requirements for optical information systems can be viewed: the more people who use a disc, the more searching value is received from the library's investment in the system. Unlike online database searching, there is no economic reason to restrict searches of optical discs. Optical disc searching of systems that employ Boolean and other powerful search mechanisms can also be used to teach online searching—without concern for online charges.

Although costs of optical systems may be fixed, they are currently much higher than for their print equivalents. Not only does the library need to invest in a subscription to the optical database, it must also buy or lease costly microcomputers and disc players. Many different print indexes could be bought for the cost of one database on CD-ROM, a fact that has far-reaching acquisitions implications. Furthermore, even though online searching costs are variable and unpredictable, a subscription to an optical information system generally costs more than most general libraries would spend on online searching of any one database.

As optical disc costs come down, the economic argument for using disc versions of print and online databases is strengthened. More patrons will search a commonly used database if they are given unrestricted access to the optical version, thus bringing down the per use cost. Searching a disc version of a database makes the advantages of online searching available to many, and thereby addresses the needs of users who cannot afford online searching.

Currentness

In general, most optical disc products are updated on a quarterly basis. Although disc mastering and replication time is diminishing, turnaround time for an updated disc is still approximately two weeks. Thus, optical discs are not the best means to get extremely current search results. Online and even some print sources offer greater currentness, as well more extensive backfiles. Many systems, however, are integrating online with disc searching. These hybrid systems, such as WILSONDISC and DIALOG OnDisc, afford users the opportunity to update disc searches by transparently dialing out to the online version, without having to execute awkward online log-in procedures; the appropriate password and dial-up protocols have already been programmed into the systems.

Search Mechanisms

As discussed in chapter 3, optical disc searching offers the most varied search options to the user: the use of windowing capabilities, Boolean searching, browse and key-word searching, and other dynamic search mechanisms provides access to full-text and bibliographic databases in a manner unattainable in print or online sources. Implications for instruction, because of these varied and complicated search mechanisms, are great: Even though searching some disc systems is fairly complicated and not self-evident to the searcher, there is no economic reason why a patron cannot spend as long as he or she needs learning the system. Librarians, however, may decide to offer formal searching instruction to patrons in order to increase the efficiency of searches, both in terms of speed of search and number of relevant citations retrieved; Linda Stewart and others at Cornell's Mann Library showed that searchers who have been given some formal search instruction do, in fact, search more efficiently than those given no training.[1] Moreover, in online searching, slow and inefficient searches cost the patron or library money, so the argument in favor of training is strong. The cost of disc searching, like that of searching printed sources, however, is not dependent on the length of time that the search takes.

Particularly in libraries where patrons have not been specially taught to search optical databases, complex retrieval modes have further service implications. While disc systems are becoming increasingly "user friendly," some assistance in searching is still necessary; therefore, librarians will want to consider location of microcomputer stations and staffing needs accordingly.

Audience

Because of the great variety of search mechanisms possible, optical disc reference sources have the potential to be the easiest for the untrained user to search. Not all disc products, however, are designed as end-user systems for a general user population. While Information Access Company addresses a general audience with InfoTrac, other optical disc system producers and vendors seek "vertical markets," or specific user groups with unique information needs. Many systems are designed to appeal to special audiences, such as librarians or researchers in a narrow subject area. Datext, which addresses the business community, and the various medically oriented optical disc systems are examples of products for "vertical markets."

Some disc products offer searchers a choice of levels of searching complexity (e.g., WILSONDISC and DIALOG OnDisc); these systems accommodate both the novice user and the more sophisticated searcher. Other products use the same complicated search language as some online services (e.g., SilverPlatter's various products) and offer less help for the untrained searcher.

In choosing optical disc products, then, a library needs to look at both its own user population and the intended audience for the product. The specific content of the database as well as the level of search sophistication required to search the disc varies from system to system.

Number of Users

One of the greatest drawbacks to CD-ROM searching of bibliographic and other databases is that only one user can search any given disc at one time. Because of this limitation, libraries that foresee a great demand, for example, for the WILSONDISC Readers' Guide to Periodicals CD-ROM may need to acquire more than one subscription to the product in order to accommodate several users of the discs at a time. A superceded, less current disc could be run on a station instead of buying a second subscription, although not all vendor contracts allow libraries to keep superceded discs. The advantage of print sources, in this case, is that many users could search different volumes of the same subscription to *Readers' Guide* at the same time. Videodisc systems, like InfoTrac, allow more users per disc; however, because of the lack of standardization, this is a less widespread technology.

The ability to "network" several users on one CD-ROM from several microcomputers has been a feature that librarians have encouraged hardware and software producers to pursue. At the 1988 annual MicroSoft Conference, Meridian Data Corporation announced CD-Net, a CD-ROM networking system that allows multi-user remote access to CD-ROM databases through local area networks (such as Ethernet, ARCNET, and token ring networks). Online Computer Systems, Inc. is also addressing the problem of networking CD-ROMs.

Although the technology for this kind of multi-user access is now becoming feasible, the issue of database producer licensing agreements for remote access of CD-ROMs to multiple users remains in question. Database producers have been reluctant to push this kind of development in order to retain maximum control over the number of groups that can use one subscription to an optically based product. Licensing agreements, and subscription cost structures, may need to be revised for multi-user networked environments.

Optical Media versus Other Formats

Optically based sources incorporate many of the capabilities of print indexes and online databases, and can be used to augment both. In most libraries, patrons rely on print indexes and abstracts for the largest part of their bibliographic needs; if the research question is multifaceted or wide-ranging, an online search may be recommend Optical sources can be used as a cost-effective intermediate s, between print and online searching. For example, patrons doing research in psychology can first narrow the topic and refine their question using *Psychological Abstracts* and its thesaurus in print form. If they need to use more powerful search capabilities, they can search PsycLIT on CD-ROM; by using the optical disc, the researchers can spend as much time as necessary adjusting their search strategy to find relevant citations. If more current references are needed, the searcher can then do an online search of PsycAlert. A more complete retrospective search can also be done later online. Hybrid optical disc systems facilitate this movement from disc to online and back. For most patrons, however, the optical disc search will be sufficient. By comparing and contrasting optical technology to print and online sources, we see that optical discs do not really represent such a different concept in reference media. Similar comparisons can be drawn with cataloging media as well: a CD-ROM catalog shares characteristics of card, computer-output-microform (COM), and online catalogs, particularly in the areas of cost, currentness, and search mechanisms. For both reference and technical services applications, CD-ROM and other optical technologies can offer librarians and patrons the best of both print and online worlds.

ORGANIZATIONAL ISSUES AND STAFFING DECISIONS

One of the first decisions that a library must make during the implementation of optical media is determining who will manage the system(s) on a continuing basis. For the benefit of library staff, system users, and product vendors alike, it is important to establish early in the implementation process who will administer and maintain optical information systems so that there are clear lines of responsibility and so that individuals involved in acquiring, managing, and using optical systems know whom to contact when a problem arises. There are several levels of staffing needs and many options for management of optical disc stations and services.

The resolution of staffing issues will depend in large part on the established organization of the public service departments and on the existing duties of individual members of these departments. Librarians need to think in terms of seven different management and maintenance questions:

1. Who will oversee or coordinate all functions?
2. Who will serve as contact person with vendors?
3. Who will maintain equipment and supplies?
4. Who will assist patrons with day-to-day search questions?
5. Who will train searchers or construct library-supplied documentation and "cheat sheets"?
6. Who will evaluate currently used systems and recommend future selections?
7. What departments will be responsible for bibliographic control and who will monitor copyright and licensing restrictions?

As evidenced by the case studies presented in this volume, different libraries have delegated these responsibilities in different ways. Overall coordination, vendor contacts, and system selection may very well fall to the head of the reference department and/or to the online services coordinator. In another scheme, these duties may be divided between different individuals for each optical system, especially if systems will be used in diverse locations. If optical information systems are located in a separate center, student monitors or volunteers may serve to assist patrons in searching; otherwise, this function may be fulfilled by reference librarians or staff members on duty at the reference desk. Training patrons and constructing search aids could be done by the bibliographic instruction librarian, the online services coordinator, or by the person with the clearest writing style or the greatest graphic arts abilities. Similarly, microcomputer and printer maintenance should probably go to the person most comfortable with computers and a screwdriver, or to whomever is working at the reference or periodicals desk closest to the microcomputer station. Of course, if optical reference systems are not used as end-user systems but are used by librarians only, these issues will have different resolutions.

At Texas A & M University, responsibility for the Wiley Laserdisk Service was delegated to the head of the Automated Information Retrieval Service (AIRS), an online end-user searching facility. This person was asked to merge operations for optical disc and online systems as fully as possible so that the same staff would help patrons with online as well as optical disc systems.[2] At the University of Vermont, a three-member task force, consisting of the online services coordinator, the bibliographic instruction coordinator, and the student assistant coordinator, is responsible for operation of the Automated Reference Center (ARC), an end-user searching facility that offers both online and optical disc databases to end users.

Any combination of optical system staffing and responsibility will work well if it reflects the existing structure and individual strengths of a public service department. The important point is that coordination, maintenance, and instructional duties should not be left undelegated. Not only would this cause confusion for vendors, searchers, and other librarians, but it could have a budgetary impact when it is realized that more staff is needed to support optical systems. Overall success of optically based information sources in a library may very well depend on who does what for the system and its users.

LOCATION OF MICROCOMPUTER/DISC PLAYER STATIONS

After a library has acquired a laser-based information system, one practical issue that must be resolved is the location of the microcomputer and disc player. Guidelines for the number and placement of CD-ROM public-access-catalog stations will be the same as for any online catalog. It is the placement of optical reference systems that poses distinct and challenging questions. The location of microcomputer/CD-player stations can have great service implications for library staff and patrons.

Hardware and Security Constraints

The location of optical information stations may first of all be dictated by hardware and wiring restrictions of the system and of the individual library. Close attention must be paid to manufacturers' recommendations on length of cabling, type of outlet, and other technical specifications. Software producers may also have suggestions for location and set-up of the microcomputer stations.

Security should be a primary consideration in the location of a microcomputer/CD-player station, both security of the microcomputer station and the safety of the discs from vandalism. Although locking mechanisms are available for CD-ROM players, most reference systems comprise several discs (e.g., SilverPlatter's current disc and archival discs for ERIC and PsycLIT); therefore, the librarian or patron will need to change discs back and forth easily. As of yet, there is "nothing on the market that exactly fits the security needs of the CD-ROM workstation in a public access location."[3] Therefore, the library must decide how to dispense compact discs to users, whether by a librarian or by the patron, and how to make sure that the disc is not removed, damaged, or stolen. Because of the CD-ROM's small, thin size, it can easily be lost or misplaced. Patrons usually do not understand the high cost of that shiny little CD-ROM to the library. And librarians must understand that most CD-ROM vendors will not replace lost or stolen discs free of charge.

Texas A & M University has devoted a separate microcomputer/CD-player station to each of the more than 15 optical products to which they subscribe; each station, then, is secured when not in use by a locking roll-top desk.[4] Other institutions have linked many databases to one microcomputer using a daisy-chain arrangement, and then locked each player.

Managing Optical Disc Stations

In looking at the implications of placement of the CD-ROM stations, it is informative to examine the print-disc-online continuum once again. Optically based reference systems are like print sources in that the library has subscribed to the discs for a single annual fee and, therefore, the greater the number of people who search them, the more cost-effective they become. Thus, there is no economic reason for restricting use of these systems by placing them behind the reference desk or in another closely supervised area. Microcomputer stations cannot, however, be interspersed among print sources without consideration of extra library staff time necessary to help patrons use computerized systems effectively, no matter how "user-friendly" they are designed to be. Although more and more optically based reference systems are intended for the inexperienced end user, some assistance from a library staff member, usually the librarian on duty at the reference desk, is still necessary. It would be helpful, then, to have optical disc stations located near the reference desk or another staffed library location so that patrons can be assisted more efficiently.

Many libraries have found that placing optical disc stations close to the reference desk has greatly increased workload for reference librarians. During a pilot project conducted at Texas A & M University's Evans Library, reference librarians and staff were asked to monitor the end-user searching stations as well as to serve traditional reference desk duties; consequently, reference staff "became extremely frustrated because their time was so broken up that they could not adequately serve either clientele."[5] Librarians at Hahnemann University also found that reference queries increased significantly after optical disc stations had been placed close to the reference desk; the total number of reference questions increased by 20 percent, and 31 percent of all reference questions dealt with CD-ROM searching.[6]

Because optical disc systems are really microcomputer peripherals, management and maintenance of the microcomputer, CD player, and printer are also at issue when considering system placement. If the librarian or other library staff member will be changing discs, adding paper to the printer, and fixing locked keyboards, then the station should be close enough to a staff member to facilitate this.

The Power of the Technology

In addition to considering the proximity of library staff to microcomputer/CD-player stations for searching and technical assistance, libraries must also look at how the disc-based system will be used by patrons as part of the print-disc-online continuum. Even though patrons may be more familiar with print-based reference sources, the powerful attraction and inherent authority of computerized information systems cannot be underestimated. When faced with a choice between a librarian and a computer, many patrons will choose and believe the computerized system first. Recent experiences with InfoTrac bear this out: Despite the fact that InfoTrac, by design, indexes only periodicals in selected and limited subject areas, patrons in undergraduate libraries will search InfoTrac even if the subject is inappropriate for that database. Librarians' printed and verbal caveats pale in comparison to the attraction of the microcomputer screen.

It is important, therefore, to place the optical disc station where a librarian can keep an eye on it. In this way, the reference librarian can point out to the patron other sources that may be more applicable to a particular reference question than the optical database. If placement close to a librarian is not possible, the scope and limitations of the disc database should be clearly outlined for the potential searcher.

Other Locations

Even though the most logical location for bibliographic databases may be in the reference area, either at the reference desk or in the reference stacks, other locations in the library should be considered, depending on the nature and content of the optical system.

A general periodicals index that is very easy to use, such as InfoTrac, may be placed in the periodicals area where most of the periodicals cited are housed. Other optical systems, such as Books-in-Print Plus, that cite monographic titles could be placed near the library catalog. Still other systems may be most effectively placed in academic departments or departmental libraries; for example, a disc version of ERIC could be offered in the Education department of a university. In general, many of the same placement issues that are faced for printed sources apply to optical disc systems as well.

Even though most of Texas A & M's optical databases are located in one area, some databases were placed nearest to the collections to which they provide access. ERIC and Newsbank, for example, have been placed in the Microtext Department, which houses the ERIC document collection and backfiles of newspapers; the LePac government documents database is placed in the Government Documents Division.[7]

Issues of security, searching assistance, microcomputer maintenance, and disc management can be at least partially controlled by placing optical disc and other computer-based end-user search systems in a separate room or center that is monitored by either a librarian, student, or volunteer. While physical limitations may prevent many libraries from exploring this option, those institutions that can assign a distinct area to computerized bibliographic searching will maintain greater control over system use and abuse. If a separate area cannot be assigned, the "controlled situation may need to be grafted on to an existing service, e.g., a microcomputer laboratory."[8] As an individual library subscribes to more optical disc databases, the issue of how patrons select the appropriate disc will become more prominent. For example, if a library subscribes to more than one WILSONDISC database, some guidance, either in the form of signage or individual help, will be needed in order to help the patron determine which one of many WILSONDISC databases is best for his or her question. Offering these databases in a monitored center or controlled area can resolve such disc selection problems.

The issue of access and control is at the heart of microcomputer/disc player location. While some libraries may feel that disc stations should be controlled, either in a separate area or near a librarian, there are strong arguments for placing stations in public areas where users can have free access much as they have free access to printed sources. More people can take advantage of optical databases if they are in a public area, available at all times. In either case, the issue of optical system placement within the library must be considered in view of all its implications. As librarians consider conditions imposed on the use of systems, they should also keep in mind that "the more conditions that are imposed, the more likely it will be that the CD-ROM services will have to be placed in a controlled setting."[9]

CONDITIONS FOR USE

Because CD-ROMs, videodiscs, and other optical media are like print sources in that they are acquired through annual subscription rather than through per-use charges, it may not matter who uses these sources or under what conditions, any more than it matters who uses print reference sources. A microcomputer and disc player can be put in a public area, much as is the print version of *Readers' Guide*, and searched by whoever needs the information at any time. Searchers will get assistance from library staff only as they need it; librarians will be involved only as far as maintaining the microcomputer station and changing optical discs when necessary. Many libraries, in fact, treat optical media in exactly this fashion with good results. Hahnemann University library places very few restrictions on CD-ROM use and librarians have found that their fears about "unrestricted access, excessive printing, machine monopolization, and lack of total security have not been realized."[10]

Other libraries, however, have felt that, because of the differences between print and optical media, use protocols should be imposed, especially in view of the sophisticated way in which some optical discs can be searched. Who does optical disc searching, when searching can be done, and how search results are printed or saved are all questions that bear consideration.

Who Can Search?

Depending on the kind of library offering optical disc databases, librarians may choose to limit who can search these systems. Academic and special libraries need to consider whether nonaffiliated users will have access to optical media; public libraries may need to decide on age restrictions for use, depending on the complexity of the system. Unlike online end-user searching, optical disc searching does not need to be restricted because of per-use cost. Optical systems, however, do present a range of searching complexity and difficulty unparalleled in print sources; therefore, libraries may want to give certain groups of users priority in searching so that staff time spent in helping patrons is more effectively used.

Of course, optical systems do not need to be offered as end-user systems at all. Many libraries keep some optical databases for library staff use only. Products such as Books-In-Print Plus, Ulrich's, and Microsoft's Bookshelf may be kept at the reference or periodicals desk like print ready reference sources, since these particular sources are used most often by librarians to answer quick questions. Other systems, especially those more complex to search, like SilverPlatter's ERIC or PsycLIT, may be searched by a librarian for a patron, like online databases, in order to ensure more complete and accurate searches. The advantages of librarians doing disc searching for patrons are that the microcomputer/disc-player stations will be more secure, and that patrons will have more successful searches; the disadvantages are that such mediated searching is very labor-intensive for library staff and the relative cost of searches is very high.

When Can Searching Be Done?

Because only one user can search any given optical disc at one time, large libraries may benefit from offering searching on an appointment basis. During certain times of the year, such as midterm or finals periods, demand for time on the disc may be great and queuing problems could arise as potential searchers wait for a turn. Generally, users will need approximately twenty to thirty minutes to complete a search on most CD-ROM reference systems, such as on the DIALOG OnDisc and SilverPlatter databases; searching InfoTrac and "browse" modes on other systems, such as WILSONDISC, should take slightly less time. If a library expects a large number of users (more than twenty to thirty a day on one system) it will need to address queuing and scheduling issues. Librarians and staff at Texas A & M's Wiley Laserdisk Service find that during busy times they become "traffic cops, directing people to available machines, asking them to wait outside the cramped area until a machine becomes available, or setting timers to ensure that nearly everyone gets a chance on the desired system."[11] Attendant problems, such as who will take and monitor appointments, will also need to be resolved. Some queuing problems, such as those for databases that require less searching time, can be overcome by simply posting recommended time limits rather than by scheduling appointments. Eager users then tend to police each other.

Libraries also need to consider whether microcomputer and disc stations will be available for searching during all hours that a library is open. Some libraries limit use to times that reference librarians are on duty, and others keep systems available at all times. Again, except for hardware maintenance, systems could be available at all times. On the other hand, because of security problems, libraries may want to limit the hours that searching on disc is available to the times that library staff could be close at hand.

How Will Search Results Be Saved?

With computer-based reference systems, both online and on disc, searchers have the choice of whether to manually copy search results from the screen, print results on a printer, or download searches to a magnetic disk. While offering users the ability to print off results saves copying time and is, to many searchers, the most appealing aspect of computer searching, it can sometimes foster indiscriminate printing, thus wasting printer paper, ink, and other searchers' time. For these reasons, some libraries have decided to limit the number of citations that a patron can print off; in many systems, the software set-up allows for an automatic limit to citations printed off. Still other libraries have decided not to offer a printing capability to searchers at all, in which case the time allotted for searching appointments will need to be longer.

Libraries are also finding that searchers increasingly ask whether search results can be downloaded to floppy disk; if this is done, users can then peruse results in a more unpressured environment, as well as edit results to reflect standard bibliographic citation formats. Not all disc products give searchers this option, although as demand increases, most disc databases will provide downloading capabilities.

Instruction and Search Planning

One final, and controversial, condition for use may be placed on some systems in some libraries: completion of a training program or a search planning sheet. Many libraries are offering workshops or other training in disc searching, and some libraries are making this training a prerequisite of searching.

There are compelling reasons for libraries not to require or offer instruction for searching disc databases. After all, licensing is not usually required for searching printed reference sources. Unless demand exceeds time available for a database, time on disc is not a cost consideration; therefore, searchers could spend as much time as necessary learning the system "hands on" at the point that they need to search it. Furthermore, end-users catch on faster than librarians might anticipate; they have been surprised by how quickly searchers have understood simple key-word and even Boolean searching, especially as more and more patrons have previous exposure to computers outside the library or exposure to online catalogs that allow key-word and Boolean searching. Optical disc systems are also becoming increasingly easy to use as database producers address different levels of user expertise. Searchers tend to resist instruction requirements and often prefer to get training or help only if they absolutely need it and then only at the point that they need it. Finally, the cost in library staff time that it takes to design and present instructional sessions, to check search planners, and to monitor completion of these requirements may simply be too high for most libraries.

There are also strong reasons for requiring, or offering, instruction before searchers can use some disc-based products. A searcher who is familiar with database structure and search options will perform a quicker and more productive search, thereby relieving some queuing problems as well as cutting down the time that librarians will need to intervene and assist searchers. On another level, teaching patrons how to search disc products provides instruction librarians with an opportunity for general bibliographic instruction: library users who can understand and effectively search online or disc databases will also be more efficient library users overall. As more end-user online systems become available, and as libraries automate their catalogs with systems that employ Boolean and key-word searching, the ability to search databases becomes increasingly important. Furthermore, patrons will need to be able to maneuver through computerized information sources not only for academic coursework, but for finding information and doing research later in their professional careers. Teaching users to search optical disc databases provides a cost-effective means for overall database searching instruction.

During April 1987, librarians at Cornell's Mann Library studied the effects of instruction on CD-ROM database searching. They divided nearly 100 education students into four groups that would search both print and disc versions of ERIC, each group having completed different training requirements: (1) CD-ROM ERIC without formal instruction, (2) CD-ROM ERIC with formal instruction, (3) printed ERIC without formal instruction, and (4) printed ERIC with formal instruction.[12] The investigators discovered that those students searching the CD-ROM ERIC, whether trained in searching or not, found more relevant citations in less time than those searching the printed version of ERIC. Furthermore, those formally trained in searching CD-ROM ERIC retrieved more relevant citations than those not trained on the CD-ROM database.[13] The Mann Library study strongly suggests that training students in the use of optical disc databases increases the efficiency of database searching.

If a library determines that searching instruction is desirable or necessary for the disc products to which it subscribes, specific points to be taught will differ somewhat from system to system. As more and varied systems become available to libraries, however, librarians will need to address the question of what basic skills will help users search any database, no matter what the individual search language may be. Searchers must also be taught the differences between optical, online, and printed reference tools, since they do not often understand the limitations or the power of the particular medium that they are searching.[14] Understanding database structure, formulating a workable search topic, isolating main concepts, and understanding basic Boolean operators will help searchers approach any end-user system, online or on disc. Searchers may further be shown how to use special search techniques such as truncation and field delimiting, how to modify a search, and how to choose different print and display options. The command language of individual databases can then be addressed through printed reference cards and on-disc help screens.

Various methods can be used to instruct users in searching disc databases. Providing computer-aided instruction, either through help screens, through generic computer-aided instructional (CAI) diskettes or vendor-supplied tutorials, or using expert systems, can be most easily integrated into departmental routines with the least amount of ongoing librarian intervention. Workbooks and other printed documentation can also be used. The most successful instruction, while also the most labor-intensive for libraries, is through workshops or individual help. Patrons, however, seem to prefer instruction that allows them to learn at their own pace and convenience: At the University of Vermont, 80 percent of users have preferred the CAI/workbook training option to workshops for searching instruction. Once patrons receive some form of instruction, contact with trained searchers by librarians will be minimal.

In addition to, or instead of, formal search training, some libraries suggest that patrons fill out a search planning sheet before they use disc products that require an understanding of more complex searching techniques (see Figure 16). These search planners may also be reviewed by a librarian or library staff member before a searcher goes on-disc. Search planning sheets lead patrons through their searches and encourage them to use printed reference sheets, database thesauri, and other guides before they do the actual disc search. These worksheets can serve as a means to cut down search time as well as to minimize librarian assistance.

The decision to train patrons in optical disc searching and the methods to be used in training depend ultimately on an individual library's staff resources, on the complexity of the systems used, as well as on the library's overall philosophy toward bibliographic instruction. Certainly, not all disc databases should require training. In

Figure 16: Sample Search Planner

_____Ref. Libn.has reviewed; _____diskette download; _____40 citations waived
****

SEARCH PLANNER
BAILEY/HOWE LIBRARY AUTOMATED REFERENCE CENTER

IF YOU WILL BE SEARCHING BRS/AFTER DARK, KNOWLEDGE INDEX, YOU MUST HAVE THIS
FORM REVIEWED BY A REFERENCE LIBRARIAN. REVIEW IS ADVISABLE FOR WILSONDISC'S
WILSONLINE/EXPERT AND SILVERPLATTER AS WELL.

1. State your search topic as completely as you can:

_____

_____

_____

2. Select the database(s) and service that best covers your topic. The ARC
monitor can provide a list of databases.

   Database(s): _____ Service: _____ __

3. Think about your topic and circle the two or three most important
different parts, or concepts, above.

4. Write each concept you circled in a top space, then list synonymous or
related terms, if applicable. If a thesaurus is available for your database,
use appropriate terms from it also.

        First Concept   Second Concept   Third Concept

   _____   _____   _____

   OR_____   OR_____   OR_____

   OR_____   OR_____   OR_____

   OR_____   OR_____   OR_____

   Connectors: _____   _____

5. Insert the connectors AND, OR, NOT, or others specified by the service
between the concepts above to combine them into a search statement.

6. Write out the search statements you will enter to get your first sets:

        1._____

        2._____

        3._____

        4._____

7. What command will you use to logoff the system? _____

ASK THE MONITOR FOR HELP WITH THIS FORM AND WITH SEARCHING!!!

some special libraries, where searchers are familiar with print indexes in a certain field and where they may have already done some online searching, no training or support may be necessary. In any case, librarians should consider administrative implications as well as long-term instructional goals when deciding what kind of searching support should be offered or required.

The requirements and conditions for using optical disc products will vary from library to library. Budgetary conditions, staffing levels, and library philosophy will all affect how any individual library will offer optical information sources. As much as possible, libraries should outline and plan for conditions of use before products are offered to the user population.

STAFF TRAINING

As libraries introduce new technologies that are primarily for patron use, staff training is as important to address as patron training in order for optical system implementation and continuing operation to go smoothly. Librarians and other staff who will have contact with optical databases must be comfortable with most aspects of system use. It is especially important for those staff members who will be in the library during times that regular reference staff may not be around, e.g., evenings, weekends, and holidays, to be familiar with each optical system.

All public services staff who will have any contact with CD-ROM and videodisc databases should be specially trained in both technical aspects of microcomputer/CD-player management and database searching techniques. First of all, staff should be familiar with the microcomputer keyboard; they should understand what operation special keys execute in each database, such as function and cursor movement keys. In addition to knowing how to change optical discs and how to restart a system, staff should also be able to "trouble shoot" hardware problems, including printer jam-ups and microcomputer system break-downs. In addition to the technical operation of microcomputers, staff should understand the details of searching individual optical databases. When patrons have questions about search software intricacies, staff should be prepared to help them with their searches. Like patron training, staff training should include sessions on database structure, Boolean searching, and other searching techniques. Finally, library staff members should know the location of user aids, such as thesauri and reference cards, as well as know how to call for library or vendor-supplied help.

Hahnemann University librarians require extensive staff training for anyone involved in the public use of optical discs. In addition to a hardware skills seminar, reference and circulation staff attend one-hour training sessions on each database followed by one-on-one review sessions with training librarians.[15] While Texas A & M University does not provide group staff training, librarians have constructed an extensive AIRS/Wiley staff manual that outlines policies and procedures for new staff members that is to be read before one-on-one training and practice.[16]

SEARCH AIDS AND ONSCREEN HELP

The extent and quality of vendor-supplied search aids and onscreen help for optical disc systems, as discussed in detail in chapter 3, have some service implications. Ideally, a patron should need only help screens and other onscreen search aids in order to successfully complete a search, with only occasional reference to printed documentation or "cheat sheets." Few systems, however, supply self-sufficient help screens or appropriate printed documentation; most libraries should therefore plan on supplementing vendor-supplied manuals and help sheets with some of their own signage and customized reference cards. As a library acquires more and more end-user systems, both online and optical, users will need both general system outlines and individual database descriptions in order to select a database. Librarians at the University of Vermont use a locally developed subject key-word guide to end-user databases to aid patrons in database selection. Texas A & M librarians have devised one- to two-page sets of instructions for each database that are kept in plastic folders by each station; they have also created keyboard templates to facilitate individual system use.[17] Staff time and the cost of materials for these user aids should be taken into account when libraries plan for optically based end-user systems. LOEX, the Library Orientation-Instruction Exchange in Ypsilanti, Michigan, is collecting library-created optical system documentation for distribution to interested libraries; before generating their own printed support, libraries can contact LOEX (c/o Eastern Michigan University Library, Ypsilanti, MI 48197, (313) 487-0168) or regional bibliographic instruction councils, for sample documentation.

While some additional printed material may need to be provided by the library, librarians nonetheless should be careful not to overdocument optical systems or to overburden the optical station with too many signs. Searchers do not usually read many signs and posters, especially those placed on computer terminals, and the more signs that are put up, the less likely it is that a searcher will read any one sign. The number and importance, then, of each sign should be carefully weighed. As with any library information campaign, those in charge of administering optical systems should plan on periodically adjusting and reworking signage and printed reference materials as systems and users change.

BIBLIOGRAPHIC CONTROL

Issues surrounding the decision of whether to catalog optical discs will be addressed here in view of the question of whether the library considers optical discs more like printed sources or more like microcomputer software diskettes. Because some optical systems correspond in content to printed indexes and abstracts, such as the WILSONDISC Readers' Guide or the range of SilverPlatter products, optical discs may be processed like their print counterparts, either cataloged separately or as added copies in a different format.

Optical discs, however, are like the various software packages that a library may acquire, in that they come out in sequential versions, or updates, that replace the earlier version. Optical information systems also include magnetic "floppy" diskettes that contain most of the retrieval software needed to run the optical system. The disc and diskette, then, together form the system, each being updated and replaced at different times; this poses additional challenges for those responsible for technical processing and bibliographic control.

For the library just beginning to grapple with the issues of cataloging, classification, and bibliographic control of optically based information, initial guidance may be found in *Guidelines for Using AACR2: Chapter 9 for Cataloging Microcomputer Software* (ALA, 1984); otherwise, precedents set by magnetic media may help to place optical media in context.

Copyright and licensing restrictions must also be considered for optical disc sources. As with online databases and services, some optical systems contain information and search mechanisms that fall under copyright guidelines; for others, the information contained on the disc may be in the public domain while the search software itself is copyrighted. Thus, a subscription to an optical system may have a detailed contract that specifies conditions for returning superceded discs and for downloading. Some system vendors do not require that libraries return outdated discs when the updated disc is received. Other vendors sell old discs to users for a discounted fee, while still others insist that all previous discs be returned to them before an updated disc will be released. In any case, close attention must be paid to individual restrictions. As the ability to network several users onto one disc becomes a reality, the issue of licensing and use restrictions will become even more important for the optical system vendor and user alike.

IMPACT ON OTHER LIBRARY OPERATIONS

As discussed earlier in this chapter, the introduction of optical media into reference and other library departments will have an impact on department administration, staffing levels, reference or service desk time, and on bibliographic instruction programs. These systems also have service implications for departments other than the public services department in which they are housed.

The expense and rapid proliferation of CD-ROM and videodisc databases make them especially problematic for acquisitions and collection development librarians; printed indexes and other sources may need to be cancelled in order to make room in the acquisitions budget for optically based titles. Also, as more databases become available from more than one vendor (e.g., the availability of ERIC from SilverPlatter, OCLC, and DIALOG), the basis for making database selection decisions extends beyond that of cost and becomes a collection development decision based on quality of search software design. As patrons find references on optical disc periodical indexes to articles in journals not owned by a particular library, acquisitions departments may also feel some pressure to acquire new journal titles.

In addition to selection matters, ordering, receiving and initial processing may be delegated to departments other than those in public services. Acquisitions or systems departments may be responsible for acquiring optical discs and making sure that the order is complete and intact.

Interlibrary loan, periodicals and microforms departments may all see the impact on their operations of the introduction of optical disc indexes. Use of library-owned periodicals and microforms may increase significantly due to the ease of searching and printing of citations from optical sources; staffing and hours of operation may need to increase for these departments. Similarly, since searchers can access so many citations more easily than they could using printed sources, interlibrary loan requests may increase. Verification of interlibrary loan requests becomes easier when patrons can search a computerized optical database rather than manually search through printed indexes to verify an ILL request; the University of Vermont found a 173 percent increase in the use of computerized databases to verify requests after optical disc searching had been instituted. Quality control in the individual optical product, however, will dictate the accuracy of those citations. Early versions of InfoTrac, for example, included many "ghost" or inaccurate bibliographic references that caused frustration for interlibrary loan and library periodicals departments.

The question of whether optical discs can be checked out of the library by users may seem to be moot at this point, since few individuals have access to CD-ROM disc drives in their homes. As optical technology becomes more affordable and popular, however, circulation issues will also need to be resolved. If and when patrons want to take discs out of the library, the security and safety of optical discs will be an added concern. The expense of a particular disc, the library's ability to replace it, and the demand for use should determine whether it can circulate or should remain in-house only.

In addition to library staff, maintenance and janitorial staff will be involved in optical systems. The administration should determine who will clean and attend to microcomputer/player stations, in order to avoid inadvertent damage. With some systems, special maintenance instructions and warnings may need to be given to cleaning personnel.

SPECIAL PROMOTION TO THE USER COMMUNITY

Optical disc-based information sources afford libraries a wonderful opportunity to increase visibility and refresh the user community's interest in the library. Library patrons have most likely heard of the new computerized information technologies through television, newspapers, other print media, and through their professional associations. Inviting users into the library to try some of these technologies, such as optical discs, further establishes the library as a place to keep up with new information sources. And since optical discs become more cost-efficient as more people search them, it becomes especially compelling to promote optical sources. Libraries should plan, then, on advertising these systems to the general user community as well as to special user groups by using printed flyers, local news articles, and special demonstrations. A library newsletter can be a good vehicle for featuring particular optical databases or services. Publicity can be as important to the success of an optical disc searching program as staff or patron training.[18]

OPTICAL SYSTEM USE EVALUATION

To facilitate service and selection decisions, libraries might plan on establishing some evaluation mechanism for optical systems from the start of their implementation. Paper-based evaluation forms are the easiest to construct, although it is difficult to get users to fill out paper forms after they have experienced the convenience and speed of computer searching and printing. Texas A & M librarians found that many patrons would not fill out paper questionnaires completely and thus evaluation results were incomplete.[19] Compiling the information from paper evaluations is also tedious for the librarian.

More efficient is the use of onscreen evaluations that are presented to the user before and after a search. Until recently, it was difficult to move smoothly from the optical disc's software to the microcomputer's operating system, which is necessary in order to create an on-disc evaluation mechanism. Increasingly, however, optical system producers are making available software that can move from the optical disc system to the microcomputer's own hard disk without rebooting the microcomputer. As a result of this facility, the patron can easily download searches and manipulate them with word-processing and database management software. This same capability can be used to create locally programmed evaluation mechanisms. Some vendors, such as Information Access Company and SilverPlatter, are also proposing to offer their own on-disc evaluation formats so that libraries can give them feedback on system use.

Although paper-based and on-disc evaluations provide the most complete information, other forms of evaluation can also be used to replace or supplement these. Librarians or other staff members can report their observations after looking on during patron searching. One-on-one interviews with patrons immediately after a search, or telephone interviews later, can also be used to gather more impressionistic feedback. Librarians can analyze search strategies and search results from copies of search planners and from print-outs of search results to follow the process that patrons used in planning and executing their searches. In any case, formal or casual evaluation procedures can influence a library's decisions on future optical database selection, patron training, and use protocols.

CONCLUSION

In "Looking Backward—CD-ROM and the Academic Library of the Future," Bruce Connolly paints a high-tech picture of a future library in which optical disc players have replaced book stacks and entire collections are accessed by a keystroke.[20] While much of his vision will certainly come to pass, today's libraries must grapple with the many implementation issues that need to be resolved before optical technologies can be offered to the public. The ways that optical systems are implemented and evaluated within any given library depend greatly on the nature of the library offering the system, the specifications of the system itself, and the type of searcher expected to use the system. Libraries should try to fit optical systems smoothly into existing service patterns while at the same time acknowledging the technology's inherent unique qualities and challenges. Planning out some details of service and use before optical systems are offered to end users or library staff will avert many implementation problems and ensure an easy integration with existing library sources and services. Even so, librarians should be aware that optical systems, as a new and developing information technology, will pose problems and delights that cannot be planned for. Service procedures and policy decisions should be fluid and easy to adjust as the realities of optical disc searching become evident.

A CHECKLIST OF SERVICE CONSIDERATIONS

The following checklist outlines questions that libraries considering offering optical disc databases to the public should examine in order to effect successful implementation.

Answers to many of the questions listed in the following checklist will vary from optical disc system to system and thus should be addressed separately for each product being introduced. Existing library policy for end-user database searching, bibliographic instruction, collection development, circulation, and the overall treatment of microcomputer disks should also be considered for each product.

Other similar implementation checklists include Diane Strauss's "A Checklist of Issues to Be Considered Regarding the Addition of Microcomputer Data Disks to Academic Libraries" (*Information Technology and Libraries* June 1986, pp. 129–132) and "Planning for End-User Searching: A Checklist of Questions" prepared by the RASD MARS Direct Patron Access to Computer-Based Reference Systems Committee of the American Library Association (1987).

I. Administration and staffing
    A. Who will manage or coordinate all functions necessary for public use of the optical system?
    B. Who will serve as contact person with the optical product vendor?
    C. Who will maintain computer equipment and order supplies?
    D. Who will take appointments for use, or who will monitor patron queuing?
    E. Who will assist users with day-to-day search questions?
    F. Who will teach searchers, both staff and patrons, how to select and use the system?
    G. Who will construct library-supplied documentation and signage?
    H. Who will publicize new systems and services?
    I. Who will evaluate optical system use?
    J. Who will recommend future product selections?
    K. Who will be responsible for bibliographic control?
    L. Who will monitor copyright and licensing restrictions?
II. Location of optical disc stations
    A. Where will players, microcomputers, and printers for each system be located?
        1. Near the reference desk
        2. In the reference stack area
        3. In a separate room
        4. In the periodicals area
        5. Near the library catalog
        6. In a departmental, branch, or subject library

    B. Does the location provide adequate security for the station?
    C. Can the location support wiring and power requirements?
    D. Is there enough work space around the station?
    E. Is the lighting adequate for computer work?
    F. Will optical disc searchers be disturbed by surrounding noise? Conversely, will searchers disturb others working in the area?
    G. Will searchers need frequent assistance from library staff? Can those staff assigned to assisting users easily get to the station?
    H. Does the location provide room for expansion or additional stations?
III. Conditions for use
    A. Who can search the system?
    B. When can searching be done?
        1. During what times will searching be offered?
        2. Will searching time be limited for each user?
            a. Who will make and monitor search appointments or time limits?
    C. How will search results be saved?
        1. Will a printer be available?
            a. Will there be a limit set on how many citations can be printed at one time?
        2. Will downloading of search results be permitted?
    D. How will multiple discs be dispensed to searchers?
IV. Instruction and search planning
    A. Do users need instruction in order to search the optical system effectively?
    B. Will instruction be optional or mandatory?
    C. What form will instruction take?
        1. Workshop
        2. Workbook or worksheets
        3. Computer-aided instruction
        4. Individual instruction at time of search
            a. Librarian to searcher instruction
            b. Peer instruction
        5. Combination of above
    D. What will be taught to searchers?
        1. Understand database structure
        2. Formulate workable search topic
        3. Assign a subject area to the topic
        4. Isolate two or three main concepts
        5. Use special search techniques, such as truncation and field delimiting

6. Understand Boolean operators AND, OR, NOT
7. Modify a search
8. Choose different print and display options, including downloading, reformatting citations, etc.
E. How will optical disc instruction fit with existing bibliographic instruction programs?
F. Will presearch planning be recommended or required?
V. Staff training
  A. Which staff members need to be specially trained?
  B. Who will train staff?
  C. What will staff need to be taught?
    1. Keyboard orientation
    2. Search software intricacies
    3. Changing discs and restarting system
    4. Hardware troubleshooting
    5. Database structure and differences between systems
    6. Location of user aids, including toll-free help number
VI. Search aids and onscreen help
  A. Will vendor-supplied documentation need to be supplemented?
  B. What printed search aids are needed?
    1. Quick reference sheets
    2. Signs on or around the optical disc station
    3. Booklets
VII. Bibliographic control
  A. How will optical discs be cataloged and classified?
  B. How will copyright and licensing restrictions be handled?
  C. How will optical systems be ordered and processed upon delivery?
  D. Will optical discs be allowed to circulate?
VIII. Effect on other library operations
  A. What voice will departments other than reference have in the selection and implementation of optical systems?
  B. What effect will optically based reference sources have on these departments?
    1. Acquisitions
    2. Collection Development
    3. Library Systems
    4. Cataloging
    5. Interlibrary Loans
    6. Periodicals
    7. Microforms
    8. Circulation
    9. Maintenance/janitorial

IX. Publicity
   A. Will the optical information system be specially publicized to user groups? How?
      1. Mailings
      2. Demonstrations or open houses
      3. Posters
      4. Local media coverage
X. Optical system use evaluation
   A. Will the optical system use be evaluated formally? How?
      1. Paper-based evaluation forms
      2. Verbal interviews
      3. On-disc evaluations
      4. Observation
      5. Analysis of search strategies and results
      6. Follow-up telephone calls
   B. What role will user evaluations play in future system selection?

REFERENCES

1. Stewart, Linda, and Olsen, Jan. "Compact Disk Databases: Are They Good For Users?" *ONLINE* 12 (3) (May 1988): 52.

2. Jackson, Kathy M., King, Evelyn M., and Kellough, Jean. "How to Organize an Extensive Laserdisk Installation: The Texas A & M Experience." *ONLINE* 12 (2) (March 1988): 57.

3. Graves, Gail T., Harper, Laura G., and King, Beth F. "Planning for CD-ROM in the Reference Department." *College & Research Libraries News* 48 (7) (July/August 1987): 399.

4. Jackson, 53.

5. Jackson, 57.

6. Silver, Howard. "Managing a CDROM Installation...A Case Study at Hahnemann University." *ONLINE* 12 (2) (March 1988): 62.

7. Jackson, 56.

8. Crane, Nancy, and Durfee, Tamara. "Entering Uncharted Territory: Putting CD-ROM in Place." *Wilson Library Bulletin* 62 (4) (December 1987): 29.

9. Crane, 29.

10. Silver, 63.

11. Tucker, Sandra L., Anders, Vicki, Clark, Katharine E., et al. "How to Manage an Extensive Laserdisk Installation: The Texas A & M Experience." *ONLINE* 12 (3) (May 1988): 38.

12. Stewart, 48.

13. Stewart, 52.

14. Glitz, Beryl. "Testing the New Technology: MEDLINE on CD-ROM in an Academic Health Sciences Library." *Special Libraries* 79 (1) (Winter 1988): 32.

15. Silver, 62.

16. Tucker, 39.
17. Tucker, 39.
18. Tucker, 42.
19. Tucker, 44.
20. Connolly, Bruce. "Looking Backward—CDROM and the Academic Library of the Future." *ONLINE* 11 (3) (May 1987): 56–61.

Chapter 5
Technical Services
Considerations

All systems have certain things in common. The concerns with software design and documentation described in chapters 3 and 4 apply to technical services systems as well as public service systems. This chapter focuses specifically on features of optical systems unique to technical service operations.

ACQUISITIONS SYSTEMS

The acquisitions systems currently on the market are in an early stage of development; they are designed primarily for preorder searching, electronic transfer of orders to selected suppliers and/or printing of orders, and, in some cases, fund accounting. The LaserSearch system, for example, allows check-in of orders received and fund accounting of up to 200 funds. Companies offering some variety of acquisitions support are Bowker, Ingram/Library Corporation, Baker & Taylor, Blackwell North America, and Brodart.

The Ingram and Bowker acquisitions systems, the most developed systems, are designed at present as stand-alone order and fund-accounting systems. They allow for electronic transmission of orders to selected suppliers. The Ingram system also interfaces to the Bibliofile cataloging system, so that materials received can also be cataloged. There are no interfaces yet to the national networks, such as OCLC or RLIN, or to local acquisitions systems, which would enable already existing bibliographic records to be downloaded into the acquisitions system or acquisitions records to be overlaid by a bibliographic record during cataloging. These acquisitions products, then, are niche market products aimed at smaller libraries that are not utilizing national networks and/or are not able to afford larger integrated systems. Bowker has announced that it will develop interfaces in the future between its CD-ROM acquisitions system and local systems. Given the complexity of such interfaces, however, due to the variety of local systems and practices, these CD-ROM systems should be evaluated based on their existing design features at the time of system selection, not on promised interfaces. Two source databases are used by the acquisitions systems. The Ingram LaserSearch utilizes Library Corporation's ANYBOOK database, whereas the Brodart PC Rose system, Baker & Taylor's BaTaSystem, Blackwell's PC Order Plus, and Bowker use Bowker's CD-ROM Books-in-Print Plus. Frequency of update of the source databases and reliability of source information from publishers would be important in evaluating the systems for preorder searching.

CATALOGING AND RETROSPECTIVE CONVERSION SYSTEMS

Just as with other automated cataloging systems, a library should utilize a system which allows the library's local database to be maintained in the MARC-II communications format. The arguments for using MARC format are no different for CD-ROM systems than for online systems or computer-output-microform (COM) systems. The MARC-II communications format allows data to be transferred from one system to another using a nationally recognized data format maintained and documented by the Library of Congress. Lack of standardization for the input and output of bibliographic records limits the library's flexibility of choice for future systems or cooperative efforts. In most cases the library also will want to use the cataloging records in an online catalog or CD-ROM public catalog, which are likely to be based on a MARC record as well. Thus, use of the MARC record establishes compatibility between systems.

Search capabilities of the cataloging system are directly related to the ease of finding records in the source database. Common search keys are title, author/title, LCCN, ISBN, ISSN, and GPO number. It is important to know whether other MARC fields are indexed or whether key word or Boolean searching is possible. Retrieval of difficult materials, such as music and classics, can be extremely frustrating if the MARC fields for uniform titles or alternate titles are not indexed.

Hit rates both for preorder searching and final cataloging will vary considerably by system, depending upon the contents of the source database(s). Consequently, the source database(s) should be evaluated separate from the hardware and software features of the system. Hit rates for online networks such as OCLC or RLIN should be compared to the hit rates for the CD-ROM systems. Even if an optically based system is considerably cheaper than the online network, this is false economy if the hit rate is so low that much more original cataloging will have to be done locally.

PUBLIC ACCESS CATALOGS

Features of particular importance to a public access catalog are search capabilities of the system, screen formats and help messages, availability of authority control or cross-references, frequency of update, and ease of establishing local parameters. A system that allows for several levels of search logic, from simple menu-driven to complex key-word or Boolean logic, will be most appropriate to a broad base of patrons. The system should enable users to instruct themselves as much as possible, since its use will be high volume and characterized by great variation in user sophistication. A search using a controlled thesaurus or subject headings and cross-references to the appropriate form of entry (name and subject) will often yield different results from a key-word or Boolean search. Thus, it is highly desirable to have both thesaurus control and key-word searching in the search logic.

Since CD-ROM is a read-only technology, the inability to update the discs frequently has been one of its most serious drawbacks as compared to online systems, both for timeliness of information in the online catalog and for workflow in catalog maintenance. Marcive first experimented with the use of a WORM drive for its laser catalog as a means of updating the library's catalog more often than is practical with CD-ROM. However, because prices remained higher than anticipated for the WORM drives and they were difficult to obtain, Marcive changed its strategy. By October 1987, Marcive demonstrated its new CD-ROM catalog which can be updated using the microcomputer's hard disk drive. The search software first queries the CD-ROM drive and then the hard disk drive. The results of the queries are combined into one result on the CRT display; thus, the fact that the system is searching both drives is transparent to the user. Library Corporation's Laser Catalog also can be updated monthly on a hard disk between complete cumulations of the CD-ROM catalog. The strategy being used by Marcive and Library Corporation is the same as that of indexing vendors such as Wilson: Back files are produced on CD-ROM for local searching and newer items are updated by online system access until the next CD-ROM disc is produced. The virtue of using the microcomputer hard disk for the local catalog is that telecommunications charges are eliminated. This mixing of media to obtain the best features of each (cost-containment using CD-ROM and currentness using the hard disk drive or online access) will become more and more common.

The frequency of update of the CD-ROM discs will determine annual production costs. Thus, the fewer times per year that the CD-ROM catalog has to be remastered and copied, the lower the annual production costs. The ability to combine the use of CD-ROM for older titles and hard disk for newer titles or record updates can have a major impact on the currentness and annual costs of one system versus another.

TERMINALS AND DISC DRIVES SUPPORTED

A number of technical-services systems which mount large, retrospective data bases have this feature: They can daisy-chain up to four CD-ROM or videodisc players to one microcomputer, so that the entire database can be searched with one query, regardless of which disc contains the data. General Research Corporation announced in 1987 that it could daisy-chain up to five disc drives, and that it will be able to daisy-chain up to 32 disc drives in the future.[1] This is particularly important for large source databases in acquisitions or cataloging, or for large public-access catalogs, where removing discs and replacing them constantly would be detrimental to speed, service, or the security of the discs.

For acquisitions or cataloging systems, the ability to support several terminals off one set of discs improves the cost-effectiveness of the system, since a number of staff members can utilize the database simultaneously. The LSSI Spectrum 400/800 series, for instance, can have up to six terminals accessing one database simultaneously.[2] The same would be true of large public-access catalogs that exceed one disc.

CATALOGING AND INDEXING OF CONTENT

The organization of and access to the content of optical discs pose the same problems to catalogers as they do for microfilm collections. The disc may contain only one bibliographic entry, as in the case of an indexing publication such as ERIC. However, it may also hold hundreds of titles which are unique bibliographic items. Producers of discs should be encouraged to include a bibliographic record for each title on the disc. Libraries should be encouraged to add these bibliographic records to the national bibliographic utilities such as OCLC, RLIN, WLN, and UTLAS, if other libraries are to be able to locate these items for interlibrary loan purposes. Because the information is electronic, it is possible to transmit the data electronically from one user to another, but one still has to know who actually owns the title and disc first.

Those who are looking at full-text applications are divided about the necessity or wisdom of indexing the text by traditional methods of thesaurus control. Joseph Howard, director of the National Agricultural Library, has stated his hope that the availability of keyword and Boolean search logic will eliminate the need for formal indexing, resulting in reduced labor for and quicker processing of collections.[3] Knowledgeable people, such as Mary Ellen Jacob of OCLC, believe that some intervening level of organization will be necessary, and that the level of relevant retrieval on full-text databases will be unsatisfactory without some additional level of searching, such as indexing terminology or abstracts.[4] As a consequence, one objective of the evaluation process for the National Agricultural Text Digitizing Project, a joint project of the National Agricultural Library and the University of Vermont Libraries, is the comparison of searching by subject headings as well as key-words versus by key-word only. MARC-II cataloging records and controlled vocabulary subject headings will be included for each title to facilitate the comparison of search results.

REFERENCES

1. Campbell, Brian. "Whither the White Knight: CDROM in Technical Services." DATABASE 10 (4) (August 87): 33.

2. Campbell, 26.

3. Conversations between Nancy L. Eaton, Joseph Howard, and Pamela Andre concerning plans for the National Agricultural Text Digitizing Project, 1987.

4. Conversations between Nancy L. Eaton and Mary Ellen Jacob concerning plans for the National Agricultural Text Digitizing Project, 1987.

Chapter 6
Hardware and Software
Considerations

Electronically based information systems are only as good as the equipment and software that support them. The design of retrieval software has been described in chapter 3. This chapter concentrates on work station components, multi-database and/or multiple-work-station configurations, system software to load and operate the system, and interface software that can aid the user in selecting databases or switching out to online systems.

COMPONENTS

Work stations are made up of components, as described in chapter 1. They typically consist of the following:

- Microcomputer with minimum 512K memory
- Floppy and hard disk drives for retrieval software, simulation software, and front-end software aids
- Optical disc drive(s): WORM, Digital Videodisc, CD-ROM
- Cards or interface boards for disc drives, printers, graphics representation, and compression/decompression
- LaserData (or equivalent) interface for digital videodisc to perform analog-to-digital translation
- Monitor (monochrome, color, or high-resolution for graphics)
- Printer (preferably laser, due to quantity of text to be printed; high-speed laser recommended for high-resolution graphics printing)
- Modem (to dial out to online systems)

Plug-Compatibility versus Integrated Work Station

A company that does systems integration makes a marketing decision whether to design its work station to be plug-compatible or to be a fully integrated work station sold as a total package, often with unique features. For the library, there are virtues and drawbacks to each approach.

A total workstation design offers the following virtues:

1. The library does not have to make any decisions about the hardware configuration.
2. The work station can incorporate nonstandard features that may be more efficient or elegant than off-the-shelf components.
3. The components can be hidden in specially designed cabinets to minimize access by the public and, thus, to provide maximum system security.
4. Maintenance is provided by the vendor, who is responsible for all components.

A drawback may be that the vendor's unique features do not meet industry standards, thus eliminating the possibility of running other vendors' discs and software on that work station. Since the vendor must provide all components, the library has no option to buy at lower educational discounts from standard hardware manufacturers. Maintenance from a small vendor who is trying to cover a national market and servicing nonstandard equipment may result in repair delays (and when the equipment does not operate, the information on the discs is simply not accessible).

Plug-compatibility means that each component stands alone and connects to other components via electrical cords and plugs that meet industry standards, such as the RS232 interface, male-female connectors, and specified pin configurations for plugs. Where industry standards exist, the library can choose to purchase only from vendors who meet those industry standards. Designing around plug-compatible components has many virtues:

1. Each component can be purchased separately, thus allowing the library to purchase from the cheapest source.
2. As hardware components are improved, the library can purchase improved components separately, replacing only portions of a work station rather than the entire configuration.
3. If local maintenance is more available and/or better and/or cheaper for one manufacturer's products than another, the library can choose a component based on that local consideration.
4. As industry standards continue to evolve, a library can choose to support those vendors who meet standards.

Plug-compatible work station design does, however, place more burden on the local library to have staff competent to choose hardware; to install and connect the various components; to provide local troubleshooting and know which component may be faulty when hardware or software problems occur; and to take more responsibility for maintenance contracts and even shipping out components for repair. Where academic institutions provide campus maintenance for microcomputers, or where certain hardware manufacturers have local plants and parts inventory, that local maintenance arrangement may be superior to vendor support or to shipping hardware off site for repair.

Compatibility and Standards

As mentioned in chapter 1, hardware standards for CD-ROM and CD-I are now defined and in the process of being implemented by most hardware vendors. However, since software development still is very fluid, software vendors may not yet take these standards into account. Thus, if a library wishes to purchase components different from those proposed by the vendor, it would be wise to try a test disc on that equipment before making such a purchase. Vendors should be willing to provide a test disc for such purposes. Digital videodisc lacks both hardware and disc standards; thus the library should not deviate from the hardware proposed by the vendor.

GATEWAYS AND NETWORK ACCESS

The migration from a single dedicated work station per database on CD-ROM to a multipurpose work station which can access back files of several databases on CD-ROM and current updates to those databases via online services is in progress. The WILSONDISC products are examples of this development. The switching from the CD-ROM database on the in-house drive to the online database requires installation of a modem in the microcomputer and front-end software which allows the user to select which database (CD-ROM or online) he or she wishes to search. The front-end software then either calls up the CD-ROM drive and search software or auto-dials the user out (with passwords supplied in the software and not visible to the user) onto the packet-switching network and into the database service desired. Some software even allows the user to save the search structured on the CD-ROM database and transfer it automatically to the online update of that database.

MULTISTATION AND JUKEBOX DESIGN

As the number of optical databases increases, the concept of one work station per disc being searched is not an adequate long-term approach to service. Dr. Anne Woodsworth, associate provost and director of University Libraries at the University of Pittsburgh, has expressed this very well:

> Our campus is wired; our on-line public catalog is available through the campus network to any terminal or workstation on/off campus. A subset of our database has been put on optical disk for use in selected medical libraries as a part of a medical informatics delivery system. Our next goal is to provide related information data bases through the campus network. Therefore, I have begun to negotiate with vendors and local libraries how we can provide local area (either campus or regional, or even smaller pc based networks within a building) access to information services. The constraint of one user per one database is not satisfactory for large interconnected computer environments in research universities.[1]

Various methodologies are surfacing as possible solutions to this need to access multiple databases from many multipurpose work stations. One involves mounting heavily used databases on local mainframe computer systems with connections on the campus network, so that anyone connected to the network can access the database online. This assumes that the volume of use will be so high that current CD-ROM and digital videodisc systems will not be sufficient to meet the search volume, since with these systems only one user can access the database at a time. Carnegie-Mellon University and the Georgia Institute of Technology are experimenting with this approach. Development of optical digital data (ODD) discs for use with mainframe computers would offer an optical storage technology alternative to electromagnetic disk drives at lower cost, with a possible trade-off of slower access times. Cornell University is pursuing experiments with use of ODD discs for large data bases on the local mainframe. Figure 17-A illustrates this approach.

A second method is to attach multiple CD-ROM disc drives to a microcomputer, with a different database or several discs for one database mounted on the drives, and to then attach that dedicated microcomputer to the network and let it act as a gatekeeper for searches coming across the network. Figure 17-B illustrates this concept, which SilverPlatter has proposed. In early 1988 Meridian Data Inc. announced its CD Net, which uses a similar approach. Each CD Net supports one to three CD-ROM drives and includes appropriate network interfaces for installation on existing LANs. CD Net comes in three models—Ethernet, Token Ring, and ARCNET—and supports a variety of local area network software. A variant of this option is SilverPlatter's proposed Multiplatter configuration, in which four microcomputer boards are mounted in one cabinet, each with up to four CD-ROM disc drives attached. The patron would dial a different number for each database, which would connect him or her to the specific microcomputer for that database, which may reside on up to four disc players. Figure 17-C illustrates this concept.

A third method is to utilize a dedicated local area network within the library for the work stations and disc drives. Online Inc. is marketing a local area network of up to four work stations connected by a small dedicated local area network (LAN) to up to sixteen CD-ROM drives holding different discs; the LAN can also be connected to other local area networks for access outside the dedicated LAN (see Figure 17-D). Whether using stand-alone work stations or any of these three shared-system approaches, once the number of discs exceeds the number of drives, the library is faced with selectively placing the most-used discs on the drives and treating other discs as reserve material to be checked out and placed on an available work station/drive(s).

A fourth approach which addresses the servicing of large collections of discs is the development of jukeboxes of discs attached to a network; with this arrangement, multiple searches on various discs can be executed as in a time-share system. The Library of Congress Data General system designed by Integrated Automation uses a jukebox design. (See Figure 10, chapter 2.) That system is proprietary, however, and still uses a mechanical arm to move the disc onto a read head, which has disadvantages of mechanical wear. Jukeboxes from major hardware manufacturers such as Philips, Sony, or Hitachi appear to be several years from being commercially available. This lack of a 100-disc-plus capacity jukebox for the CD-ROM discs is affecting the ADONIS project, in that libraries do not wish to receive more than about one new disc each week, given that the discs must be loaded manually until a jukebox is available.[2]

All of these proposed solutions must deal with the problem of contention. First there is contention of work stations coming across the local area or campus network to the device, followed by contention for a specific disc on the device(s). Since access time to data on a CD-ROM is slower than for electromagnetic disk drives, the contention problem is potentially more severe than in an online environment and will challenge designers of hardware and software.

It is critical that producers of optical systems recognize the need for housing and servicing large numbers of discs and work quickly toward solutions. Libraries will purchase additional work stations up to a point, but limitations of funds will eventually place a cap on purchases of CD-ROM databases and full-text publications until the hardware-management bottleneck is solved.

Figure 17: Network Conceptual Design

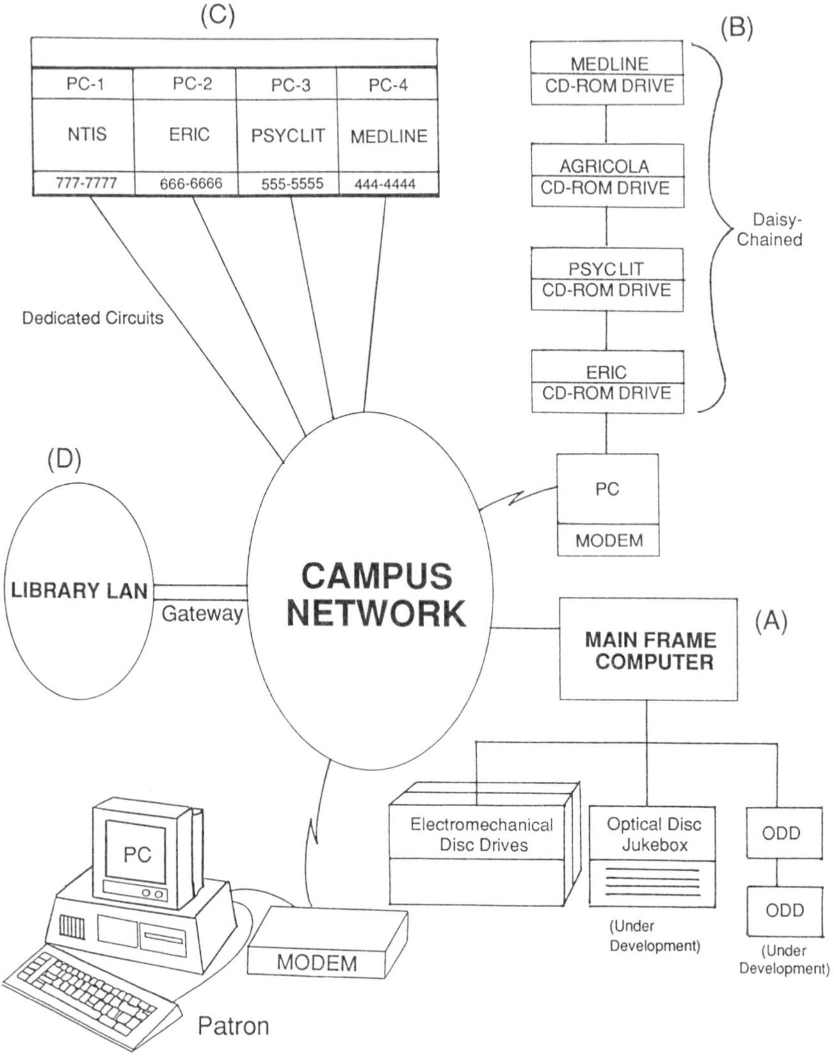

(C)

PC-1	PC-2	PC-3	PC-4
NTIS	ERIC	PSYCLIT	MEDLINE
777-7777	666-6666	555-5555	444-4444

(B)

MEDLINE
CD-ROM DRIVE

AGRICOLA
CD-ROM DRIVE

Daisy-Chained

PSYCLIT
CD-ROM DRIVE

ERIC
CD-ROM DRIVE

Dedicated Circuits

PC

MODEM

(D)

LIBRARY LAN

Gateway

CAMPUS NETWORK

MAIN FRAME COMPUTER

(A)

Electromechanical Disc Drives

Optical Disc Jukebox

ODD

(Under Development)

ODD

(Under Development)

PC

MODEM

Patron

INSTALLING THE SYSTEM

For librarians who have little exposure to microcomputers or other peripheral equipment, the prospect of setting up a system may be quite daunting. However, experience at the University of Vermont indicates that one should not fear so long as one can read directions and is patient and methodical.

Typically, all components ordered arrive in separate boxes and must be unpacked and assembled. The various interface boards come separately boxed and must be installed in the microcomputer; just follow the printed directions. Thus, you may be faced with taking the case off the microcomputer to insert the various boards. UVM's experience has been that manufacturer and vendor directions are sufficient and do not assume previous experience with such hardware. It is advisable to read all of the instruction manual sections and information sheets concerning component assembly and installation before beginning to work. This is one situation where reading the instructions is vital. Most manuals and instruction sheets contain detailed line drawings to accompany every step of the assembly process. The AT&T user's manual has such instructions and drawings explaining how to open the case and install additional boards safely and correctly. Some systems, such as the Compaq II Plus portable, will require special screwdrivers or other small tools, which are usually available from the local computer supplies store.

Software is received on floppy disks which usually must be loaded onto a hard disk drive. A basic knowledge of the Disk Operating System or DOS commands is very helpful to understanding the instructions for copying software files and creating subdirectories. This knowledge can be learned by reading the DOS manual which accompanies every microcomputer, or by attending a class or workshop offered at a computer store, school, or college. However, vendors have made software installation extremely simple. SilverPlatter, for example, has the user insert the floppy disk and type "install." A series of menus appears on the monitor, each with detailed instructions on how to select such variables as the make and model of printer and CD-ROM drive and the databases that will be played on the work station, and how to decide whether the number of citations that can be printed at one time should be limited. Other vendors' setup selections may be more complex. When installing WILSONDISC, the user must specify telephone numbers of packet-switching networks and passwords for auto-dial, work file names, and similar choices that configure the system for hardware.

Occasionally there are options which may not be obvious. Two examples come to mind. With Dow Jones News Retrieval's access through an academic password, the searcher can access a full-text database (for which there is an extra charge), but that enhancement is enabled by the Dow Jones staff rather than within the install program. This capability is not stated in the documentation, yet the capability exists. On the other hand, WILSONDISC includes unlimited access to the corresponding online database for only the cost of the telecommunications access fee. However, access to all of the other WILSONLINE databases is allowed with the user's password, but at the standard connect-time rates, unless the password is disabled from accessing those other databases.[3] It would be possible for a patron to run up large search fees without the library knowing it, if this capability to access all WILSONDISC databases—regardless of whether the library had the CD-ROM subscription—were overlooked during installation.

HARDWARE AND SOFTWARE UPGRADES

Because publishers and vendors are still refining their software for database retrieval from CD-ROM or other optical drives, it is common for them to send out improvements in the software on a floppy disk. The user must load those changes into the system. It is likely that these systems will have to be updated on a regular basis. Correspondingly, documentation will also have to be updated and distributed to users.

While software upgrades require continual attention, hardware upgrades have a larger financial impact. The need to change hardware comes from two directions. First, software may be improved to the point that more memory or additional storage is required. SilverPlatter's early products ran on a standard IBM PC with two floppy disks. Now both a floppy disk for loading the programs in and a hard disk for operation are standard. Few programs can run on less than 512K memory and a hard disk.

The second contingency affecting hardware occurs when a manufacturer makes a major design change, such as IBM did in 1987 with the announcement of its new IBM PS/2 microcomputer. The design of the new micro is quite different from that of the earlier IBM PC, AT, or XT—and is in fact not compatible. That announcement had three effects. First, libraries about to purchase equipment wanted to know whether to purchase the old PCs or to wait for the new ones. Vendors had to decide whether to rewrite their software to run on the new hardware and to decide how long to take in making that software investment. Finally, as IBM phased out production of the older PC, libraries that wanted to proceed with purchase had to select PC clones and find ways to provide adequate maintenance for them. This same thing is happening with CD-ROM disc drives: Newer drives may have multiple capabilities for graphics, sound, and motion. If a library is to be able to use products aimed at the improved drives, they may have to upgrade old drives or even eventually replace them. This problem of obsolescence in a rapidly changing environment will forever be with us, as long as we look to technologically based information systems.

WORK STATION ERGONOMICS

It is important to plan an environment for the work station(s) which is comfortable for the user. If the work station configuration is not conducive to serious work, it will result in low productivity and use, as well as complaints. Ergonomic factors which should be taken into account include:

- Lighting to reduce glare from the CRT screen.
- Work station desks at the right keyboard and monitor height for comfortable typing and reading.
- Chairs which offer adequate back support and movement to and from the work station.
- Monitors which can be moved and tilted to suit individual heights and eye reading levels.
- The color of the monitor background and contrast to reduce eye strain.
- The securing or tying of electrical cords and cables to minimize loose cords which might pose a hazard to the work station user or people working or walking in the area.

While these admonitions seem self-evident, a tour of most libraries housing automated systems or optical systems will reveal a grave inattention to these details.

REFERENCES

1. Woodsworth, Anne. Letter to Nancy L. Eaton, April 30, 1987.
2. Campbell, Robert M., and Stern, Barrie T. "ADONIS—A New Approach to Document Delivery." *Microcomputers for Information Management* 4(2) (June 1987): 95.
3. Tenopir, Carol. "Costs and Benefits of CD-ROM." *Library Journal 112* (14) (September 1, 1987): 156.

Chapter 7
Fiscal Considerations

PRODUCT PRICING

The area of optical publishing with the most confusion and least guidance is that of pricing. Publishers are not yet consistent or agreed on how to charge for optical systems, either as compared to competing print, microform, or online versions or according to fair market value. Thus, new products coming on the market tend to be priced on the high side and to begin to come down in price only with competition, when there is more than one source for the same product. Two examples of this are ERIC and MEDLINE. ERIC is available from at least three vendors: SilverPlatter, OCLC, and DIALOG OnDisc. The original price for ERIC from SilverPlatter in 1986 was $4,000 per year for the current and archival discs. When OCLC announced it was offering ERIC with its CD450 software for considerably less in 1987, SilverPlatter countered by dropping its price the same month. Each producer offers value-added features which it hopes will persuade you to choose its version, of course. Each has different retrieval software. Each has packaged ERIC slightly differently and priced it accordingly. For instance, OCLC's ERIC is also accompanied by a disc of the educational titles in the OCLC union catalog (EMIL). DIALOG OnDisc allows you to update files by searching online. SilverPlatter hopes that the large number of databases which can be searched with their software will encourage libraries to select their version of ERIC as well as the other databases which SilverPlatter offers. The January 1988 pricing for ERIC, taken from price lists from these three vendors, makes plain the variation that can occur (see Figure 18).

Similarly, MEDLINE is now available from at least a dozen CD-ROM and online vendors. Again, competition has kept the price down. Other value-added features which distinguish one MEDLINE product from another include the ability to run on an Apple MacIntosh computer rather than IBM and the ability to conduct a hierarchical search of MeSH subject headings.

Figure 18: Price Comparisons*

	Silver-Platter	OCLC	DIALOG OnDisc
Current disc with quarterly updates	$650		
Current disc with annual update	$390		
Archival disc set	$900		
Complete starter set			
	$1,200 plus 650/yr after the 1st year		
Current ERIC (1981- present, quarterly updates, online search between updates			$950
Complete ERIC (1966-present, quarterly updates, online search between updates			$1,650
Complete Education Series: ERIC (CIJE & RIJE) & EMIL with quarterly updates		$995 (member) $1,095 (nonmember)	
ERIC (1982–present, including current ERIC disc, CIJE, & RIJE)		$350 (member) $425 (nonmember)	
ERIC Retrospective Files		$750 (member) $900 (nonmember)	
EMIL (OCLC holdings)		$300 (member) $350 (nonmember)	

*Prices are subject to change.

Publishers are worried about losing profits from their existing products when they release optical versions of the same data. They also feel compelled at present to maintain all previous formats, since only a small percentage of their total customers are currently prepared to buy the optical version. They also worry that their volume of sales will go down on the paper, microform, or online version, thus increasing per-unit costs of production, at the same time they are trying to recover their development costs for the optical version. For that reason, the CD-ROM version often is not an exact match of the original version, but a subset or variant edition. For example, the

CD-ROM version may lack graphics and illustrations. This encourages the library to continue to take both versions; some publishers give a discounted or linked price if the library continues to use both versions. For instance, a subscription to a CD-ROM database from WILSONDISC includes unlimited access to the corresponding online database. Psychological Abstracts offers 10 percent discounts for multiple subscriptions to their CD-ROM product and a 10 percent discount for subscribers to the printed index.[1] Before cancelling a print version in favor of a CD-ROM format, be sure to compare the content of each format to see whether they differ.

In general, publishers have not been very understanding of the hardware dilemma that libraries face. For example, where there is even a break for multiple-copy subscriptions, the discount for the second copy ranges from about 10 percent to 25 percent. Given that most of the subscriptions are in excess of $1,000 per year—and that the main reason for needing a second subscription is the one-disc-per-work-station limitation of current hardware, more realistic pricing for added copies is desirable. Libraries would be more likely to distribute a second copy to a subject department or library if the price were reasonable. Very few libraries have the resources to take a second copy of a $2,000 per year title at a 25 percent discount just because the disc can only be used at a single work station. This is one instance in which pricing the added copies much lower, say 10 percent of the original cost, and selling many more copies to more libraries, might generate more revenue than the higher copy price to fewer libraries. Many publishers still harbor the expectation that the bulk of their major profit will eventually come from selling directly to the individual user; thus, they are reluctant to lower the costs for added copies, which might discourage individuals from buying directly. If experience with online searching is an indicator, however, the individual information user is not equivalent to a mass-media consumer and will have an upper limit in mind on what he/she will spend. Just as libraries have remained the largest users of online databases, except in very narrow niche markets such as law, medicine, and business, that is likely to be the case for optical databases as well. George E. Hall, vice president of Slater Hall Information Products, a producer of census data and government statistics on CD-ROM, found that the major base of installed CD-ROM disc drives is libraries and has reoriented marketing to take this into account.[2]

In order to encourage more rapid market growth, many CD-ROM producers are now offering group discounts through regional library networks such as NELINET and AMIGOS. SilverPlatter and WILSONDISC, for example, offer such discounts. Thus, a library should check with its local network for the possibility of such favorable pricing.

Licensing Agreements

Unlike printed indexes or monographs, which are owned outright by the library, or pay-as-you-go online databases, "CD-ROM databases are usually [obtained through] a subscription lease arrangement. Libraries purchase permission to use a CD-ROM database, not the discs themselves. Under this arrangement, if a current subscription is canceled, all discs must be returned to the publisher. Thus, libraries will no longer have access to retrospective information on disc if they cancel their current subscription."[3] Exceptions to this practice are WILSONDISC, which does allow the library to retain previous discs as long as it does not sell them, and PAIS, which allows the library to keep the last disc received when a subscription is canceled.[4]

Mastering Copy Costs versus Production Costs

Manufacturing costs for a CD-ROM disc master and copies have dropped dramatically in the last three years, mainly because of the opening of new production plants in the United States. Costs quoted in the SAIC contract with the University of Vermont in July 1987 were $7,000 for the glass master and $10 per copy for 100 copies.[5] Since then prices have dropped further, with a master under $3,500 and copies for $7 or less, depending upon quantities. One company announced mastering for $1,500 and copies for $2 as of June, 1988. How, then, does a publisher justify charging thousands of dollars for a CD-ROM subscription? Part of the rationale is "what the market will bear," but total production costs and initial start-up investment in developing and marketing new products should also be taken into account. As described in chapter 1, the production process includes data capture, conversion, pre-mastering, encoding and mastering, and distribution. Preceding these steps, of course, is the editorial process. Even so, knowing the actual production costs for CD-ROM allows the librarian to evaluate whether the total price of a CD-ROM publication seems reasonable. Comparison of prices for different versions of public databases provides the user with a measure against which the usefulness of each product's unique features can be judged. With proprietary databases, when prices seem excessive, the only alternative is to shop elsewhere and to select a different product that comes close to accomplishing the same objective, or to decide not to purchase. In a few instances, libraries have been successful in banding together, as with network discounts.

Average Search Costs: CD-ROM versus Online

The major cost benefit of CD-ROM databases as compared to online searching is the library's ability to budget for fixed costs and to lower the average search cost by increasing volume of use on the fixed-cost service. Data collected at the University of Vermont Bailey/Howe Library for the period September–December 1986 showed a per-search average of $3.16 for CD-ROM databases (ERIC and PsycLIT), as compared to a per-search average of $7.12 for end-user dial-out services (BRS/After Dark, Knowledge Index, WILSEARCH) and $18.40 for online mediated searches by librarians. The average can vary considerably, depending upon the databases used and the number of searches per database in any given month. For example, the average cost per search on ERIC for the month of October 1986 was an astoundingly low figure of 85 cents, based on 368 users logging 184 hours. This compared to a monthly prorated cost of $312.50 for the service. Equally important, ERIC received 184 hours of use by end-users in one month, as compared to 33 hours for the entire fiscal year (FY 86) for mediated searching by librarians. Thus, many more patrons were reached by the CD-ROM service.[6]

Newer figures collected by the Bailey/Howe Library during the fall of 1987 are consistent with the early findings. The average search charge for ERIC/CD for the month of October 1987 was $2.40, compared to the average cost of $18.20 for an online search. Total searches conducted on end-user and online services by the end-users themselves totaled 770 in October 1987, as compared to 83 mediated searches conducted by librarians.[7]

HARDWARE: BUNDLED SUBSCRIPTION OR SEPARATE COMPONENTS?

Most vendors offer bundled subscriptions, which include both the database subscription and hardware. Hardware is usually offered at full cost and spread over two to five years as a lease/purchase. Libraries pay more to purchase hardware this way than with outright purchase, but it does allow them to treat the subscription from their acquisitions budget and, if necessary, to spread the cost over several years. This may be the only funding available to some libraries. Another virtue of purchasing hardware, particularly CD-ROM disc drives, this way is that the vendor purchases in quantity and therefore often has drives available. An individual library dealing directly with the manufacturer might have to wait in a purchasing queue, since production of disc drives often lags behind demand. A comparison of a lease/purchase versus outright purchase of a Hitachi drive from SilverPlatter illustrates the cost savings possible with direct purchase.[8]

- Direct purchase by library from manufacturer: $500–700
- Payment in advance (90-day warranty) from SilverPlatter: $785
- Payment in advance (one-year warranty) from SilverPlatter: $885
- Direct purchase from SilverPlatter (90-day warranty): $855
- Direct purchase from SilverPlatter (one-year warranty): $955
- Two-year lease/purchase from SilverPlatter at $550/yr: $1,100

Libraries qualify for educational discounts for most equipment, including microcomputers and disc drives. Most campuses have special arrangements with microcomputer vendors at significant discounts of 25 to 40 percent. Thus, most libraries in this situation will save considerable money by purchasing separate components. It is critical, however, to insist on equipment that is compatible and to include these technical requirements in the purchase request, so that the purchasing agent does not foist off on the library an incompatible component.

As libraries go beyond CD-ROM data base subscriptions and begin to build collections of CD-ROM discs which they own, they will be forced to take responsibility for configuring equipment to take a variety of hardware requirements into account. At that point, the bundled purchase becomes less and less attractive, since the library will be absorbing responsibility for configuring and maintaining equipment far beyond a specific publisher's system requirements.

Costs of a Typical Work Station

A typical work station configuration includes, at the minimum, a microcomputer, hard disk drive, floppy disk drive, CD-ROM drive and interface card, printer and interface card, and modem. Prices should continue to decline; thus, hardware costs should continue to drop slightly.

Sample Configuration[9]

AT&T micro with 640K memory, color monitor, 20MG hard disk, floppy disk (PC clone)	$2,200
Epson FX86e printer (near-letter-quality)	500
Modem (Leading Edge)	150
CD-ROM drive	805
	$3,655

REFERENCES

1. Tenopir, Carol. "Costs and Benefits of CD-ROM." *Library Journal* 112 (14) (September 1, 1987): 156.
2. Conversation between George E. Hall and Nancy L. Eaton, January 12, 1988.
3. Tenopir, 156.
4. Tenopir, 156.
5. Contract between Science Applications International Corporation and the University of Vermont and State Agricultural College, July, 1987.
6. Eaton, Nancy L., and Crane, Nancy B. "Integrating Electronic Information Systems into the Reference Service Budget." *Reference Librarian* 19 (1987):165–166.
7. Bailey/Howe Memorial Library, University of Vermont and State Agricultural College. Computer-Assisted Reference Service Statistics: October 1987.
8. SilverPlatter Price List, 12/87.
9. Actual prices paid by University of Vermont during 1987, including educational discounts and based on campus contracts.

Chapter 8
The Future: Policy
Considerations

As members of a profession, it behooves librarians to look beyond the microscopic concerns of implementing a new technology—specifically, optical technology—and to envision the total context within which that technology will operate. If electronic information delivery is changing the nature of the way people use information and, therefore, the nature of the library, we must first envision that future, then help shape it. We return, then, to the question posed in the preface: Which technology for which application? Optical technology is one in a continuum of information-delivery mechanisms, from online to paper. What are the policy implications of that continuum?

THE INFORMATION-DELIVERY INFRASTRUCTURE

The future information environment will continue to provide access to all formats of publication. Figure 19, which had its early conceptualization in a presentation by Don Willis of University Microfilms, Inc., at the Library and Information Technology's Preconference on Optical Technology in July 1986, depicts the components of that information environment. The heart of this environment is a sophisticated workstation with access to a whole host of attached peripheral devices and outside databases, vendor systems, electronic mail systems, and electronic document delivery services. Still prominent, however, is the need to access paper and microform collections, based upon location information found in citation and bibliographic databases. It becomes obvious that optical technology must be viewed as one component in a larger information-delivery network, not simply as stand-alone work stations and databases. Viewed in the larger context, the systems currently on the market are very early versions of a much more sophisticated environment which is still evolving. Pat Battin, in her testimony before Congress in 1985, summarized this very succinctly:

Figure 19: The Delivery Mechanisms

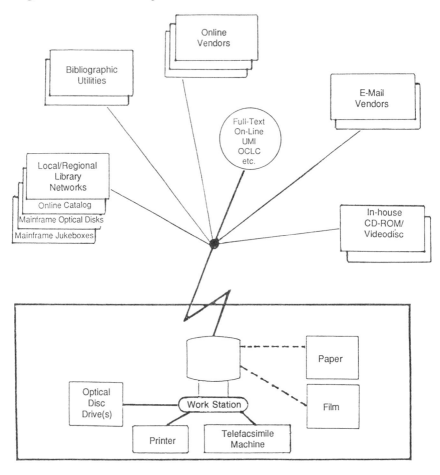

Contrary to futuristic predictions, the electronic communication systems and capacities have supplemented, not supplanted, the traditional means of communication. The peer-reviewed scholarly journal remains the primary means of communicating scientific research results. There is no indication at present that scientists are prepared to accept electronic formats as a substitute for printed materials. The need for linkages between formats is paramount. The expansion of new information sources and tools creates incremental expenses for the university and requires a new information infrastructure to meet the demands of scientists, who want both books and databases, libraries and electronic networks.[1]

The Report of the Commission on Freedom and Equality of Access to Information, commissioned by the American Library Association to examine the future implications of information technology, likewise stresses the need for a new infrastructure:

Electronically stored and delivered information requires an infrastructure comparable to that existing for the bibliographic control of printed materials. This is an enormous task and will require imaginative leadership, wide cooperation, and public support. It is an endeavor, stretching over years, that should be a major objective of the American Library Association and the National Commission on Libraries and Information Science, with enlarged public funding for NCLIS.[2]

Elements which are impacting on policy development as this electronic infrastructure emerges are extremely complex. Central to the infrastructure is the definition of "access to information." Following receipt of the commission report, the American Library Association appointed a special Committee on Freedom and Equality of Access to Information, charged to analyze the commission report and to suggest action appropriate to the American Library Association. In carrying out that charge, the committee conceptualized "access to information" graphically.[3] Figure 20 illustrates the dynamics between the individual's education and skills, geographic and physical access to systems and services, technological innovation, public policy, law and regulations, etc. Key issues which require attention have already begun to emerge, including: the impact of deregulation of the telephone industry on educational and public institutions, with the possible need for special educational rates and a research telecommunications network; the effect of one's ability to pay for information upon one's ability to meet educational requirements, conduct research, or participate as a citizen; the need for school systems and libraries to participate in "information literacy" programs, in order to help citizens learn how to use new information technology; and bibliographic control expanded to the article or chapter level to support electronic document delivery.

Telecommunications Networks

At a time when information retrieval and dissemination are becoming more and more dependent upon telecommunications networks, deregulation of the telephone industry has complicated access enormously. The rates for digital transmission continue to increase without any regard to preferential educational rates, thus threatening to make data transmission unaffordable for many educational institutions and libraries. (The Washington Office of the American Library Association participated in a coalition of public organizations which presented evidence and testimony to the FCC during 1986 and 1987 on the effect that rate increases would have on libraries' use of electronic networks, causing the FCC to withdraw certain proposals for rate increases on data transmission.) The other major effect of deregulation has been to encourage campuses to install local tele-

Figure 20: Information Access

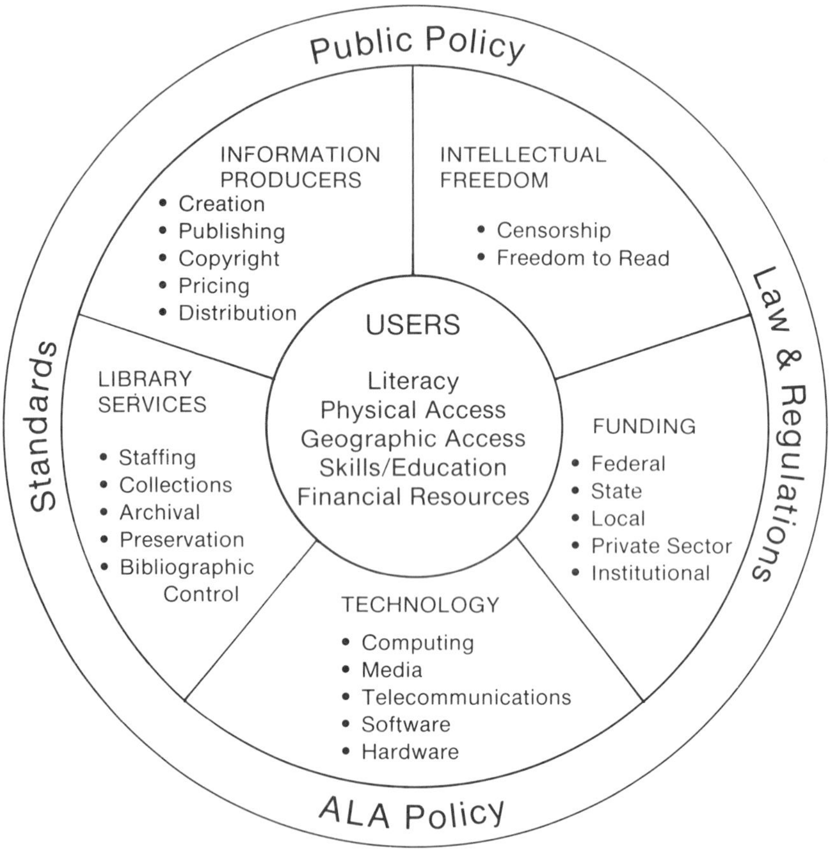

INFORMATION PRODUCERS
- Creation
- Publishing
- Copyright
- Pricing
- Distribution

INTELLECTUAL FREEDOM
- Censorship
- Freedom to Read

USERS
Literacy
Physical Access
Geographic Access
Skills/Education
Financial Resources

LIBRARY SERVICES
- Staffing
- Collections
- Archival
- Preservation
- Bibliographic Control

FUNDING
- Federal
- State
- Local
- Private Sector
- Institutional

TECHNOLOGY
- Computing
- Media
- Telecommunications
- Software
- Hardware

Public Policy

Law & Regulations

Standards

ALA Policy

(Reprinted by permission of J. Dennis Day, Chair, ALA Special Committee on Freedom and Equality of Access to Information)

phone systems and local area networks to save money, with little regard for meeting standards which would facilitate networking.

Archiving and Cataloging Electronic Data

With regard to optical technology specifically, no policy exists as to how the masters for CD-ROM discs and videodiscs will be archived for the future. At present, the masters remain at the disc manufacturing plant, not even with the publisher. The industry already distributes back files on static discs and updates only the most current disc. Who will take responsibility for the permanent retention of the back files, whether on the master discs or in electronic data bases? At what point is a static disc considered an edition, not to be changed further? At what point is a file which is continually being updated considered worth cataloging? Will libraries take responsibility for cataloging electronic publications and seeing that these entries are added to the national databases such as OCLC, RLIN, and UTLAS for resource sharing? It has become almost a cliché that libraries are no longer concerned with ownership of information, but rather with access to information. Access requires the knowledge that the information exists and can be shared.

PRIVATIZATION OF INFORMATION: THE "VALUE-ADDED" DEBATE

During the eight years of the Reagan administration, there was a concerted effort to privatize the distribution of government information. "During the past six years, this ongoing chronology [prepared by the American Library Association] has documented Administration efforts to restrict and privatize government information."[4] A report prepared for the Association of Research Libraries emphasizes that "How government information in electronic format is disseminated will have an impact on existing partnerships between the government and for-profit and nonprofit institutions....Policy development for dissemination of government information is in great flux, and discussions with representatives of various government agencies suggest that there may be quite a number of approaches."[5] Pat Battin and the Association of Research Libraries have stated strong positions in support of the government's responsibility in disseminating information. Said Battin in 1985 testimony before Congress:

Since unfettered access to information sources and open communication of research results have been the hallmarks of American scientific inquiry and research productivity, I would like to focus my remarks on the new barriers to this traditional access accompanying the powerful potential of information technology. In addition, the emergence of an "information industry" which views information as a commodity rather than a public good is causing an alarming shift in the perception of value from the intellectual quality of information to a value based on short-term market demand.[6]

In this same vein, the 1987 Association of Research Libraries report focuses on the government's responsibility to disseminate information regardless of format:

While technology offers opportunities that may be to the advantage of users in both public and private sectors, political decisions about meeting government obligations to provide information should not be contingent on format. It is the nature of the information itself, its significance in fulfilling citizenship information needs and other government responsibilities, that should drive decisions about choice of format, the level of value-added enhancements supplied by the government, and about how dissemination is to be financed.[7]

A good illustration of the issue of the government's responsibility to make data available in its generic format (versus with "value-added" features which are appropriate from the private sector) is the census data. Most census data are now maintained in electronic format. Census tapes are distributed to data centers in each state; use of the tapes is a local or state responsibility. This often requires that a programmer be utilized to extract the data needed by a researcher. Even so, the data are available to the public. The Census Bureau is now demonstrating a prototype CD-ROM version of census data, which includes limited ability to extract data in set formats, similar to the standardized publications printed off the magnetic tapes for libraries. In 1987, Slater Hall Information Products began marketing CD-ROM subsets of census data that include a sophisticated proprietary search and retrieval software package. The vendor has indeed added value to the raw data by the way the data are packaged, and many libraries will opt for this version because of its flexibility. It is also appropriate for the Census Bureau to continue to make the raw data available, however, so that researchers still have the opportunity to massage and analyze the data themselves. In this way, the government can meet its responsibility, and the private sector can still have opportunities for profit based on "value-added" products.

The ARL task force report presents a taxonomy of government information systems and identifies a value-added model developed by Robert S. Taylor. "Together the value-added model described by Taylor and the taxonomy of government information in electronic forms provide mechanisms to address the four key considerations in planning for public availability of any particular information system; they may also lead to general conclusions about how certain categories of government information should be disseminated."[8]

Access: Fee or Free?

Historically, most libraries charged for online database searching when it began to be a regular service in the late 1970's. The most popular rationale for charging was that the library was "adding value" to information already available in the library in paper format. This failed to take into account that the products were (and are) not equivalent, and therefore the information provided was not the same. The other rationale was that the service was very expensive, due to the variable nature of connect times and telecommunications charges, and that libraries could not afford the service out of existing budgets. Optical technology eliminates the telecommunications charges, and optical products are priced on an annual subscription fee, so that a library can now budget for these products within its normal acquisitions budget on an annual basis. Thus, there is less and less reason to continue to charge for electronic information. A mounting concern is the effect that charging has on the intellectual enterprise. Again quoting Pat Battin:

> A major concern for scientists is the continuation of the subsidized browsing capacity in the electronic environment. The control of databases and networks by the for-profit sector has created a set of costs imposed directly on the information seeker. There is already evidence that this constraint influences the path of intellectual inquiry, the choice of research topics for the graduate student, and alarming variations in the level of potential productivity among the information haves and have-nots. Information costs have now become a visible influence in determining the thoroughness of a literature search by graduate students, a factor which erodes the overall quality of the research effort.[9]

This same concern is expressed by Dr. Douglas E. Van Houweling, vice-provost for information technology at the University of Michigan, in *The Campus of the Future:*

> Equity of access across the institution is a critical goal. Access needs to be provided to students regardless of their ability to pay and to disciplines regardless of the state of technology development. We have information that indicates that students who come from less well-to-do backgrounds benefit more by access to instructional computing technology than do their more well-to-do peers. Major advances in many of the arts are now coupled to the use of sophisticated information technology, but the support for acquisition of that technology is much less available than in the sciences and engineering. The rapid improvement in price-performance in information technology means that leadership in a particular area often goes to those institutions able to afford technology in its early stages before universal access becomes affordable.[10]

Therefore, many librarians now question the wisdom of charging for electronic publications solely on the basis of format. A major challenge to library administrators is to find strategies for incorporating core electronic information systems into annual budgets to protect the heart of the educational and intellectual process of which they are a part. This may require difficult collection and information use analysis and decisions on what materials have what priorities in funding.

Funding and Institutional Planning

Various reports to the nation on the status of our educational systems point to the fact that colleges and universities have not been spending enough on equipment. Research laboratories often are out of date and not competitive with laboratories in private industry, for instance. Unfortunately, this means that libraries must compete with other ailing units on campus for funds for the equipment necessary to electronic information systems. The same is probably true of municipal and state governments in many instances. Even so, librarians must make the argument that hardware is now an ongoing expense which must be planned for on a continuing basis. Likewise, libraries should be involved in institutional planning for telecommunications networks, local area networks, mainframe computers, and microcomputer facilities which have heavy hardware (capital) funding requirements. The critical need for this level of coordination between the library and other information/computing units is described in detail by Nina Matheson in her landmark work on information systems for academic health sciences centers[11] and in OCLC's *Campus of the Future.*[12]

CONCLUSION

The emergence of optical technology and its potential for libraries is exciting. It also brings with it mammoth policy considerations for the public-versus-private roles in information creation, organization, storage, and dissemination; for an infrastructure to support electronic information systems; for funding at the local, state, and national level; and for integrating electronic formats with prior formats. Electronic information does indeed supplement, not supplant, the traditional means of communication. While it is important for librarians to become familiar and comfortable with optical technology, those systems must be viewed in a larger context and integrated into existing services and into traditional bibliographic instruction programs. The Committee on Freedom and Equality of Access to Information views the individual (see Figure 20) as the center of the information process. That is the key to the future of optical technology.

REFERENCES

1. U.S. House of Representatives, Committee on Science and Technology, Task Force on Science Policy: Hearing, September 12, 1985. Testimony presented by Patricia Battin, Vice President and University Librarian, Columbia University. Typed manuscript: 3.

2. *Report of the Commission on Freedom and Equality of Access to Information.* Presented to the Council of the American Library Association. Chicago, American Library Association, January, 1986: 111.

3. American Library Association. Committee on Freedom and Equality of Access to Information. *Final Report,* presented at the 1988 Annual Conference (New Orleans) of the American Library Association.

4. American Library Association. Washington Office. *Less Access to Less Information By and About the U.S. Government: 2; A 1985-86 Chronology: January 1985 - December 1986* (December 1986): 1.

5. Association of Research Libraries. *Technology & U.S. Government Information Policies: Catalysts for New Partnerships.* Washington, D.C. (October 1987): 10.

6. Battin, 2.

7. Association of Research Libraries, 1.

8. Association of Research Libraries, 8–14.

9. Battin, 8.

10. Van Houweling, Douglas E. "The Information Technology Environment of Higher Education," *Campus of the Future: Conference on Information Resources.* Wingspread Conference Center, June 22–24, 1986. Columbus, OH: OCLC, 1987. 101–102.

11. Matheson, Nina W., and Cooper, John A.D. "Academic Information in the Academic Health Sciences Center: Role of the Library in Information Management." *Journal of Medical Education* 57(10, part 2).

12. *Campus of the Future: Conference on Information Resources.* Wingspread Conference Center, June 22-24, 1986. Columbus, OH: OCLC, 1987.

Chapter 9
Strategies for Implementation:
Case Studies

In the spring and summer of 1987, we conducted a mail survey asking 150 libraries to summarize their attitudes toward optical disc products and their experiences with selecting and installing them. The following nine libraries were selected from the group of 32 respondents based on the range of optical products they had tested or chosen and the observations and information they provided. They represent four different kinds of libraries (academic, school, special, and public), and reflect both public service and technical services applications of optical technology. The cooperation of all of the librarians who answered the survey requests is greatly appreciated.

For published case studies that have appeared since this survey was completed, see Appendix B (Optical Information Systems: A Selective Bibliography).

BAILEY/HOWE LIBRARY
University of Vermont
Burlington, Vermont

Type of Library: Academic
Size of population served: 10,000 faculty, students and staff
General description of user population: Primarily undergraduate, with most academic departments granting master's degrees and several offering the doctorate.
Optical information systems in use: WILSONDISC (Applied Science and Technology Index, Art Index, Biography Index, Business Periodicals Index, Education Index, General Science Index, Humanities Index, Readers' Guide to Periodicals, Social Sciences Index); SilverPlatter's ERIC, PsycLIT, and Agricola; from February 1986 - June 1987, InfoTrac.

In September 1986, the University of Vermont's Bailey/Howe Library embarked on a rather ambitious and innovative end-user search project: the Automated Reference Center (ARC). The ARC is a fully subsidized end-user search facility that integrates optical, online, and local databases. It offers university-affiliated patrons access to twelve CD-ROM databases (nine WILSONDISC indexes, and SilverPlatter's ERIC, PsycLIT, and Agricola); three online services (BRS/AfterDark, Dialog's Knowledge Index, and Dow Jones News Retrieval Service); and access to LUIS, the online catalog. From February 1986 until June 1987, the library also offered InfoTrac instead of WILSONDISC. The ARC and its patrons also serve to test and review various new optically based products.

The Center comprises three rooms located in a complex across from the reference desk. These are (1) a searching center for the WILSONDISC databases; (2) an adjoining room designated for searching the SilverPlatter discs and the online end-user systems; and (3) a third connecting classroom, containing five microcomputers and a computer overhead projection system, used for end-user training workshops, demonstrations, and individual viewing of an interactive instructional program that deals with searching theory and technique. The Automated Reference Center is open daily from 8 a.m. to 11:30 p.m. (with slightly more limited weekend hours). After completing a training program, patrons make half-hour-long appointments ahead of time to search the SilverPlatter databases and the online end-user service; no appointment (or training) is necessary for WILSONDISC or Dow Jones. A trained student monitor is in the ARC during most hours, and a reference librarian is available to answer difficult search questions and to review search strategy. There is no charge to the patron for any of the services.

Partly because the library is bearing the total cost of end-user searching, and also because the SilverPlatter optical products employ search software as complex as that used by online services, patrons are required to complete a training program in database searching before they can search any system except WILSONDISC or Dow Jones. This training requirement can be completed in one of two ways: The patron can attend a 90-minute workshop or he or she can complete a workbook and also view an instruction diskette (CAI). The patron then fills out a "search planner" that is reviewed by a reference librarian (librarian review is optional for the optical disc products). While the end-user training program has involved considerable time and effort on the part of both librarians and patrons, the results have been more cost-efficient online searches and more effective and thorough disc searches. During FY '87, over 1,000 persons were trained using both training methods.

Planning for the Automated Reference Center began during the Spring of 1986. A three-person committee comprising members of the reference department, working under the direction of the head of reference with financial and creative support from the director of libraries, was delegated to plan and implement an end-user search program with a projected start-up date sometime in September of that year. The committee was charged with five tasks to complete before the ARC could open: (1) to choose appropriate end-user products; (2) to outline protocols of use (e.g., who could use the ARC, when, how often, under what conditions); (3) to develop a training program for searchers; (4) to look at ways to evaluate the systems and to evaluate the overall success of the ARC; and (5) to order furniture, wiring, supplies, hardware, and other attendant materials.

Because the University of Vermont has large education and psychology departments that offer a range of advanced degrees, ERIC and PsycLIT were logical choices for the first optical products that the library invested in. It was also in the online versions of ERIC and PsycINFO that the mediated search service did most of its searches. InfoTrac, on trial at the library since February, was continued for one year in order to serve the needs of the large undergraduate population. During FY '88, however, InfoTrac was replaced with WILSONDISC databases. Members of the reference department felt that patrons would be better served by a more comprehensive series of databases that offered a wider range of search capabilities; consequently, the InfoTrac subscription was not renewed. Also in FY '88, Agricola was added to the SilverPlatter offerings.

For less frequently searched subject areas, the online end-user systems (BRS/After Dark and Knowledge Index) are available. Reference librarians are closely monitoring database use in these online systems in order to determine which subject area databases might be more cost-efficient for the library to acquire in an optical format. In FY '87, the business database ABI/INFORM was searched most often on the online systems; a compact disc version of this or a similar database would be a likely candidate for a compact disc at Bailey/Howe. During its first year of operation, the ARC has become a very popular and successful reference service. For FY '87, the total number of ARC searches done (except for InfoTrac) was close to 3,000, with nearly two-thirds of those done on the SilverPlatter optical discs. The average cost per search was $4.70 overall; ERIC averaged $3.52 per search and PsycLIT averaged $4.08. Of course, the more people who searched the compact discs, the less expensive each search became. Most of the searching was done by equal numbers of undergraduates and graduate students; some faculty members in education and psychology departments in fact required that their students do an ERIC or PsycLIT search as part of the course requirements.

Although an online statistics-gathering system was instituted, it did not operate properly, so figures for the total number of searches and the types of ARC users were taken from appointment sheets and evaluation forms. Reference staff and ARC monitors agree that the actual number of searches could be at least 50 percent higher than those figures, especially for the compact disc products. For FY '88, a new statistics system has been mounted on all ARC searching stations except for those running WILSONDISC databases. This new system is expected to give librarians more accurate information on the number and nature of people searching each system and on the success of each search.

End-user searching, of which optically based searches form the greatest part, has had an effect on library departments outside of the ARC itself. Interlibrary loan requests using a computer search as verification have increased by 173 percent and total ILL requests have increased by 14 percent. The librarian-mediated search service has reported 22 percent fewer searches. The interest generated by end-user searching, as well as by the online catalog, has also had an effect on bibliographic instruction; approximately one-third of the reference department's instructional efforts are being geared toward computerized literature searching. Reference librarians have also reported a significant amount of reference desk time being devoted to counseling end-users (approximately 1.5 hours over the course of an average 14-hour reference desk day). Impacts on collection development and acquisitions, while potentially significant, have yet to be formally assessed.

Librarians at Bailey/Howe are eager to continue offering new and innovative information technologies to library users. The Automated Reference Center has attracted a great deal of interest and support from the university community, bringing new users into the library and also refreshing established patron relationships.

FIDELITY INVESTMENTS INFORMATION/RESEARCH SERVICES
Boston, Massachusetts

Type of Library: Special
Size of population served: 300 (directly); 7,500 (total)
General description of user population: Investment analysts, fund managers, marketing specialists, systems managers, and staff with responsibilities in new business development and venture capital.
Optical information systems in use: Datext, Compact Disclosure, Lotus One Source, CD-Worldscope.

Cathy Stephenson and Jack Cahill at Fidelity Investments had several purposes in mind when they chose optical disc products for Information/Research Services: (1) to reduce the staff time spent doing routine searching; (2) to provide an easy introduction to financial databases for unsophisticated users; and (3) to save some of the costs of extensive online searching. A single microcomputer work

station provides access to Datext, Compact Disclosure, and CD-Worldscope. Fidelity is also testing Lotus One Source.
Datext, which was purchased in June 1986, is the product most familiar to Fidelity users and is frequently used "to provide a quick, first look at a company or industry and to organize data into a neatly sorted format. The Compact Disclosure service is not as well known nor as broadly used as Datext. . .but its search commands are much more powerful. It offers both an Easy Menu search mode and a powerful Dialog emulation mode which allows for an unlimited range of screens and reports. CD-Worldscope provides historical financial statements, fundamental analysis, and stock performance data for more than 3,000 foreign and U.S. companies." In Cahill's opinion, Lotus One Source, which combines Compustat fundamental data with a weekly supplemental stock-pricing service and several other databases, has the advantage that "the data is immediately available and goes directly to a work sheet, saving several steps. The disadvantage is in ease of use; this is not an easy system to perceive or use."
The compact disc products have generated tremendous enthusiasm among users at Fidelity and are the most popular of computerized information sources offered. However, since optical disc products are not as timely as online sources, extensive online searching is still done to complement the CD-ROM technology. Stephenson notes that the sources are also expensive. Offering optical media has reduced the use of reference publications, cut down on the amount of photocopying of reference materials, and lowered the frequency of borrowing of corporate file material. The Fidelity librarians have used an attractive library newsletter, circulated within the company, as a very effective method of advertising the availability and features of the optical disc products.

FONDREN LIBRARY
Southern Methodist University
Dallas, Texas

Type of library: Academic
Size of population served: 8,000
General description of user population: Undergraduate students in humanities, social sciences, business, education; graduate students in business
Optical products in use: InfoTrac

Fondren Library chose an optical product to "introduce new information technology into an otherwise very traditional print-oriented library and to experiment with its use and value," according to Linda Sellers, assistant director for public services. Fondren began a subscription to InfoTrac in June 1986, and has leased two IBM work stations and placed them in a "high traffic area near the card catalog and circulation and reference desks." The system is available for use during all library hours (108 hours per week), and no identification is required. There is a self-policed 15-minute suggested time limit on searches; training is not required. Fondren provides a laminated indexed list of journals beside each terminal; this list has been annotated to show which journals are in their collections. They also provide a copy of IAC's thesaurus at the terminal. The reference staff troubleshoots the system and maintains supplies.

InfoTrac has proved to be very popular with students, especially business students, and the service is heavily used. Both terminals are usually busy during peak library hours, sometimes with waiting lines. Sellers documents the following problems with the system: (1) theft of software; (2) power outage damaging the disc; (3) poor print quality because "we deliberately chose to use standard computer printer paper (for cost savings) instead of coated paper recommended."

Fondren decided to try InfoTrac for one year and now must decide whether to retain the optical product over other media, primarily microforms. The decision will be based on content as well as the characteristics of each medium in information handling. Sellers notes that InfoTrac has many advantages: speed, convenience, ability to print citations, and a multiyear database that is easy to search. The disadvantages are "cost; titles indexed not always a good match to collection; no key-word searching; and lack of Boolean logic, which is often cited as a shortcoming because our expectations have been raised by DIALOG and others. When compared with manual searching, which is slow, one-year-at-a-time and without Boolean parameters, this is a boon. We forget if we want DIALOG power we have to have DIALOG complexity (even with end-user software) and at this stage of the technology, we must choose." Sellers feels that InfoTrac should modify its software to display the subject headings and subheadings display first, instead of showing the first entry that matches the subject being searched.

It is Sellers' subjective impression that InfoTrac has increased the use of periodicals and microforms at Fondren. The library has not added periodical titles indexed in InfoTrac to the collection and has no plans to do so. ILL figures rose every month for the last several months of the survey (in the spring of 1987), but that rise cannot be traced directly to InfoTrac. Sellers believes "users of InfoTrac use it simply *because* they want instant returns, and are a totally different mind-set from those who use Interlibrary Loan." While very interested in other optical products, Fondren has no future plans to acquire more, primarily because of cost and the lack of standardization.

LOS ANGELES COUNTY PUBLIC LIBRARY
Downey, California

Type of library: Public
Size of population served: 2,889,450 (est. 1986/87)
General description of user population: One of the five largest public libraries in the country, LACoPL consists of 91 community libraries and 10 institutional libraries.
Optical information systems in use: LePac and InfoTrac

The Los Angeles County Public Library, one of the five largest public libraries in the United States, has maintained a public catalog on microfilm since 1977. By the mid-1980s, the library was confronted with numerous equipment breakdowns, splitting microfilms, and a catalog so large it required two microfilm readers. County librarian Linda Crismond lists the following advantages of optical disc products as factors in the library's decision to consider replacing the microfilm catalog with LePac: "Higher density storage; increase in access points; anticipated lower maintenance costs and more reliable service of electronic vs. electromechanical catalog in microfilm readers; future capability for transparent transfer to an automated circulation system via modem; capability to use PC-based equipment for other applications such as word processing where catalog usage is not constant; capability of using equipment to read other CD-ROM based products."

The library gave LePac a formal 90-day test early in 1986, receiving some of the first units that Brodart released. LePac stations are based on IBM PC-compatible microcomputers with single or double Hitachi compact disc drives, and offer a choice of a full keyboard (recommended for staff use) or a ten-key pad designed for patron use with Menu mode. At the test site, the Brakensiek Library, one full keyboard unit plus printer was installed for reference staff use, and four units with the simpler ten-key pads replaced microfilm catalog readers for public use. Staff and patron responses, which were carefully monitored, were overwhelmingly positive. Specifically, Brakensiek staff felt that the LePacs were "easier to use, easier to read, faster and quieter." No more instructional time was required than for the microfilm catalog, cataloging errors were easier to spot, and the printer at the reference desk was very useful. The test documented major problems with equipment breakdowns and poor vendor support; however, these weaknesses occurred because the library was one of the first sites to test the new Brodart Automation product. The library performed a second test with replaced equipment and improved software, and the results were even more successful. In fall of 1986, the library decided to begin a gradual replacement of microfilm readers with LePac workstations. By August 1987, the Los Angeles County Public Library had 80 LePacs in place among the

91 libraries in the system. Friends of the Libraries groups are helping with the purchase of LePac units and printers at several libraries. The LePac work stations are installed at reference desks and in public areas wherever the microfilm readers were placed. They are available to all users and staff, whenever the library is open. Staff training is provided by a LePac committee and staff in technical services; reference librarians assist users as needed, although Crismond notes that little help is required.

At this point in the replacement process, Crismond feels that "Both public and staff members began using [the LePacs] with very little instruction. They have found the increase in access points very useful; the ability to go directly to an author or title on the expert keyboard saves search time. Since we are able to display all holdings in the CD-ROM catalog, only one look-up is required. We have had inadequate experience (a few months) to assess hardware reliability. Vendor support has been excellent. Concerning the security of equipment, Brodart offers and we have purchased cables to secure equipment to some stationary object; the monitor locks onto the CPU unit. A front panel covers the drives and is secured by bolts so floppy disk and CD-ROM disk cannot be reached without the key, which is also required to start the machine."

The Los Angeles County Public Library's future plans include CD-ROM-based reference databases like Books-In-Print Plus, PAIS, and selected WILSONDISC indexes.

McHENRY LIBRARY
University of California
Santa Cruz, California

Type of library: Academic
Size of population served: 8,600
General description of user population: Undergraduate students (primarily liberal arts), graduate students (primarily sciences)
Optical products in use: LePac Government Documents Option

Margaret Robinson reports that the McHenry Library selected the LePac Government Documents Option, purchased in February 1987, for its combination of key-word and Boolean search capabilities. "Compared to online media, the advantages are that the meter isn't obviously running and one-on-one staffing isn't required. Students love the medium, and it serves as a 'hook' to introduce them to other systematic search techniques, online or manual." Disadvantages are (1) only one user at a time can be served; (2) there are increased equipment and maintenance needs; and (3) as a nonprint medium, it requires nonroutine acquisition and maintenance procedures.

The system is available to end users during all hours that the library is open. All categories of the library's researchers, including students, faculty, and community, utilize the service without restrictions. "Instruction in LePac use is folded into existing formal instructional sessions, as paper and roll microfilm monthly catalog instruction was handled. Most end users are introduced to the system by staff, conduct their searches, and bring printouts back to staff for retrieval. The system is so simple that it has required minimal staff training and no additional staffing."

Robinson feels that the software for Government Documents Option has some unexplained and irrational elements: for example, in expert mode, exact subject headings with subdivisions are not retrievable. The system, however, "because of the keyword and print capability, has made existing reference retrieval and interlibrary service for government publications easier; it has not increased use thus far."

MEDIA CENTER
Edmund W. Thurston Junior High School
Westwood, Massachusetts

Type of library: School
Size of population served: 300
General description of user population: Seventh- and eighth-grade junior high school students
Optical information systems in use: Academic American Encyclopedia, Bibliofile, Earth Science Laser Disk

The Media Center at the Edmund W. Thurston Junior High School began to experiment with optical disc technology in the fall of 1986, when Roxanne Baxter Mendrinos, director of library media and computer applications, developed an in-service training workshop for science teachers, focusing on laser discs and microcomputer labs. The Media Center purchased the Earth Science Laser Disk, which includes videotapes, slides, films, and still pictures on astronomy, weather, volcanoes, rocks, earthquakes, oceans and other aspects of earth science. The disc runs on a Pioneer 12-inch laser disc player and is located in the Science Department at the school, where it is used in teaching in two classrooms. Students can also search for information and visuals on their own research topics. The system is used daily and requires very little training. Although the system has searching capabilities, it is not presently being used with a microcomputer; Mendrinos plans to order software for computer compatibility this year. The laser disc has proved very popular, and social studies teachers are considering a disc on ancient civilizations, while science teachers are interested in one on physical science.

But the Earth Science disk was only a starting point for the Media Center. In January, 1987, Mendrinos purchased BiblioFile to convert the shelf list to complete MARC format records. Bibliofile, from Library Services Corporation, is a CD-ROM multiple-disc (four discs) product, which includes the Library of Congress MARC record catalog, the ANY BOOK ordering package from Ingram Book Company, catalog card production and label production. The system runs on an IBM PC and Hitachi CD-ROM player, which are located in Mendrinos's office, and available to other library media personnel for training in CD-ROM technology. Mendrinos says,

"My goal is to simulate the university experience with my students and have subject, title and author access of our collection via the computer and an automated circulation system. My shelflist is not completely in MARC format, which is the standard for automation. For a small library of 12,000 volumes, I could not afford to send my shelflist out, nor would the administration provide extra staff for the conversion project. I have volunteers, including library science practicum students, using the CD-ROM Library of Congress disk to match shelflist records and save the MARC formatted forms to floppy disk. Twenty-five records are converted per hour and in three months my fiction shelflist has been saved to disk in the correct format. Records can be edited for in-house cataloguing and original cataloguing is also possible. This CD-ROM technology has afforded my library with catalog access to the large online databases such as UTLAS and OCLC without the costs of membership and online time. I can also search the CD-ROM laser disk for ISBN numbers for books I want to order. With a modem I can order directly from Ingram Book Company through the ANY BOOK laser disk provided by Ingram in the Bibliofile package.

"The system is very cost effective. For $2,200 (not including the CD-ROM player), I can have volunteers convert my shelflist, which a few years ago would have cost $20,000 and taken two years. This will have a very strong impact on automating my library. Within the next year, I will be deciding on the circulation and online catalog system I will work with. All my records will have been converted to MARC format for efficient retrieval and tapes will be made of my collection. This will be important so that if the technology changes in the future, I will be able to input the data into another system."

In February 1987, the Media Center added Grolier's Academic American Encyclopedia on CD-ROM to its resources, which already included the print version of this and other encyclopedias and the online database version of the Academic American (through BRS Instructor). The system runs on the same IBM PC and Hitachi player that are used for BiblioFile in Mendrinos' office. Plans for 1988 include an additional microcomputer and player to provide a dedicated work station in the library. The students, who were trained in class sessions of about 45 minutes, have proved very adept at using the CD-ROM Encyclopedia. During research periods, the system is booted up in the morning and available throughout the day, with Mendrinos providing search assistance if needed. About 200 of the school's 300 students have used the Encyclopedia to date (June 1987). Since the optical disc version is not updated as frequently as the online version, 50 of the 200 students followed their CD-ROM search with an online search for more recent statistics and information. Use of the CD-ROM version has decreased online time and made research more fun for the students, and, with the online databases, has increased circulation in the Media Center.

Mendrinos describes her students' use of the Academic American Encyclopedia to do a research project in a combined English/social studies unit on Third World countries entitled "Feeding the Billions":

"Students use the CD-ROM encyclopedia, the *Academic American* online databases, encyclopedia indexes, the card catalog, the Readers' Guide, the almanac, reference sources, [and] Appleworks' databases on countries of the world to research information on their topic. Students must use the traditional sources of information before using the CD-ROM encyclopedia or online databases.

"Seventh- and eighth-grade students use both the 'Browse Entry' and the 'Word Search' strategies for researching their topics. Students use the 'word search' strategy to locate all articles in which their word appears through the twenty volumes of the encyclopedia located on the CD-ROM disc. This is very effective in finding more information on a topic, especially if the student has a related terms list.

"The 'Browse Entry' function is used to retrieve the main article on the topic in the encyclopedia. A student can type in 'Grenada,' for example, and retrieve the main article on that country. Of invaluable assistance is the ability to see an outline of the article by pressing one of the menu keys of the encyclopedia software. The outline will provide the student with the main subheadings of the article. This facilitates efficient access to key information.

"Students did not have trouble learning to use the CD-ROM software. The software is menu-driven and very easy to learn. I showed the seventh- and eighth-grade social studies classes and the seventh-grade academic development classes how to use it in a group lesson. Students came in the next day and immediately retrieved and printed their information. I will prepare step-by-step directions and have them available, but they haven't been necessary. The faculty and I are very pleased with this addition to the library and the way the students are responding and retrieving information. Before February [1987] the price of the encyclopedia was $199. It is now $299 but still a good buy compared to the printed version at $450. However, graphics are not included. Boolean search strategies and efficient access and retrieval of information make this a precious addition to our library."

For more information about Thurston Junior High School's experiences with optical products, see Roxanne Baxter Mendrinos' article "CD ROM: Research Strategies for a Lifetime," in *Media & Methods* 23 (4) (March/April 1987): 8–11.

TACOMA PUBLIC LIBRARY
Tacoma, Washington

Type of library: Public
Size of population served: 158,900
General description of user population: Individuals, businesses, local government in an urban area
Optical products in use: InfoTrac, Books-In-Print Plus/Ulrich's Plus, SilverPlatter's ERIC, Grolier's Electronic Encyclopedia, Bibliofile, WLN's Laser Cat, Intelligent Catalog.

Tacoma Public Library has in use a wide range of optical disc products, which can be divided into two groups: (1) those available to patrons and (2) those whose use is restricted to the staff. The library's public catalog was introduced for patron access in September 1987 on the Library Corporation's Intelligent Catalog. This system uses an IBM PC-compatible computer with a hard disk drive and two Hitachi disc players, and provides full Boolean searching of the library's holdings, plus key-word and standard author, title, and subject heading access. The system is currently available only at the Main Library, which has been an alpha and beta test site for the Library Corporation. The Intelligent Catalog was scheduled for installation in the branch libraries in 1988. Dalia Hagan, head of technical services, comments that, "Because the product was so recently introduced, public and staff reactions have not been officially measured and recorded. Early informal response has been extremely positive."

InfoTrac is also available to patrons whenever the library is open. Tacoma has four work stations attached to one player, and subscribes to both InfoTrac and Government Publications Index. They also purchase the Magazine and Business Collections from Information Access Company on microform to complement the service. Hagan says that "All staff have been trained to use the system, and designated individuals assist with station/printer problems as they arise. Patrons have been extremely enthusiastic about the product (it is very easy to use) and expect to find not only citations but the entire article as well. We have experienced a dramatic increase in the use of our periodicals collections (especially the back files) with the inception of InfoTrac and the Magazine and Business Collections."

For reference staff, Tacoma has an innovative "Quick Information" work station, an IBM PC-compatible with two CD-ROM players, that is used for Books-In-Print Plus and Ulrich's Plus, Laser Cat, Grolier's Electronic Encyclopedia, and SilverPlatter's ERIC. Books-In-Print Plus, purchased in 1986, is also used in technical services. As head of technical services, Dalia Hagan is responsible for training for all of the CD-ROM products. She comments, "All technical services and reference staff have been trained in its use. Reference staff use it for patron request verification, collection development, creation of bibliographies and checking of availability. Technical services staff use it for verification purposes. We may be experimenting with direct patron access to the product later this year." The system is virtually trouble-free and has an excellent vendor-supplied manual. Tacoma staff would like to see monthly updates of the database replace the quarterly ones now offered, but the enhanced searching capabilities have made this product "extremely popular with staff, especially in working with patrons." For more information about Tacoma's experiences with Books-In-Print Plus, see Dalia Hagan's article, "The Tacoma Debut of *Books-in-Print Plus*," in *Library Journal* 112 (4) (September 1, 1987): 149–151.

The Electronic Encyclopedia is used "sporadically by reference staff. Slow key-word searching makes it difficult to use in [the] Quick Information [station]. It can be valuable for searching obscure terms and finding terms in context. Some software 'glitches' cause the system to freeze." For example, key-word searching the term "clouds" locks up the machine, which must then be rebooted. Reference staff also use ERIC on the Quick Information station instead of the online version. Availability on compact disc has resulted in "more use of ERIC. Tacoma Public Library has a policy of not charging the public for online searches. Because our budget is fairly small, online searching is kept to a minimum. With the advent of CD-ROM products, we are able to provide access to these databases to the public in a more expanded manner—increasing public service in an area which was previously underserved."

LaserCat, a subsystem of the Western Library Network's database containing location and call number information, is used to locate holdings information for ILL purposes and to facilitate regional resource sharing. Hagan notes that LaserCat software is "moderately awkward to use—assumes patron has some other CD-ROM and/or WLN experience." Its availability has resulted in a "moderate increase in ILL transactions to other WLN member libraries. The majority of our ILL work is done online with OCLC."

Overall, Hagan weighs the advantages of optical products' ease of access, Boolean search capabilities, and ability to own or lease products against the disadvantages of software peculiarities of individual systems, quarterly update schedules, costs compared to print products, and the lack of technology for chaining multiple work stations. Tacoma plans to concentrate on refining the Intelligent Catalog as a patron access catalog, and is considering adding WILSONDISC indexes to its range of products.

THOMAS P. O'NEILL LIBRARY
Boston College
Chestnut Hill, Massachusetts

Type of library: Academic
Size of population served: 15,000
General description of user population: Undergraduate and graduate students, faculty, administrative and professional staff
Optical information systems in use: InfoTrac, SilverPlatter ERIC, SilverPlatter PsycLIT

Marilyn Grant, coordinator of the Computer Search Service at Boston College, decided to purchase optical products as another mode of access to a database. John Stalker, chief reference librarian, and Rhoda Channing, assistant university librarian for Library Information Resources and Collection Preservation, were interested in testing this new technology at Boston College and approved the proposal to purchase ERIC and PsycLIT. Researchers at the O'Neill Library are now able to use several versions of ERIC and PsycLIT: print subscriptions, online versions via DIALOG and BRS, an end-user version through BRS/After Dark, and the CD-ROM products from SilverPlatter. Education faculty member Walt Haney calls them "different media for different minds." Reference librarians make sure that library users are aware of the various products and their advantages; most patrons soon develop a strong preference for one medium in particular.

O'Neill Library began its experiences in optical technology with a subscription to InfoTrac in 1985. It now has four IBM PC work stations with printers located in an area behind the reference desk. The stations are not directly visible from the desk because of a floor-to-ceiling bookcase wall behind the desk. InfoTrac is available whenever the reference desk is staffed. A typical weekly schedule is Monday through Thursday 8:30 a.m.–11:00 p.m.; Friday 8:30 a.m.–9 p.m.; Saturday 9 a.m.–5 p.m.; Sunday 11 a.m.–11 p.m. Boston College students, faculty, and staff have first priority, although identification is not formally checked. There is no scheduling, but if a user spends more than one-half to one hour at the terminal and other searchers are waiting, the reference librarian will ask the user to yield and return later. The usual amount of time per search is between five and fifteen minutes. Boston College does not require training for InfoTrac, but librarians will do short demonstration searches if requested. Librarians also handle the paper refilling and system troubleshooting chores for InfoTrac.

Grant reports some initial problems in "setting up the system and getting it to run smoothly. The main problem with vendor support is the distance of Information Access Corporation [in California] from this site. Vendor support seems better now, but that is because we have had fewer equipment/software problems lately." O'Neill Library has also had security problems with InfoTrac; users have tried to get into the operating system, removed the back of the player cabinet, and rearranged cabling to the work stations.

Although it is a very popular service, InfoTrac has not caused a perceptible rise in interlibrary loans at Boston College. Grant says that students either confine their research to titles held at the college or check to see if Boston Library Consortium members hold a title and use it at a member library. *McLean's* has been the only periodical added to the collection in direct response to requests based on InfoTrac.

O'Neill Library has an uncommon work station setup for its ERIC and PsycLIT subscriptions, which were begun in January 1987. The library is a test site for SilverPlatter's MultiPlatter configuration, in which only the keyboard, display monitor, and printer are at the user's work station. The MultiPlatter unit, which can handle more than one disc, is located directly adjacent to the reference desk. The service is available whenever the reference desk is staffed. Although scheduling was not required initially, it has become necessary to have a sign-up log as the traffic has increased. Reference librarians offer very brief individual training (10 to 15 minutes per person) and will help with ongoing searches as needed. The optical products are discussed in bibliographic education classes beyond the freshman level and in BRS/After Dark training classes. A training class for SilverPlatter is being contemplated.

Grant has high praise for SilverPlatter's vendor support and feels the company, which is located in a nearby Massachusetts suburb, has been very responsive. She feels that, "Documentation on the disc and in the manual supplied by SilverPlatter is excellent. Newer versions of the system software have reduced the need for rebooting, which had to be done frequently when the product was first installed. Since this is a test situation, we expect some glitches. We have not had major security problems. We did suggest a design modification of the unit—namely, a door on the front of the control panel."

Based on her experience with optical products at the O'Neill Library, Grant feels that their "major advantage has been to library users. With the SilverPlatter products, they are able to conduct a real literature search (employing Boolean operators and other search limitations) without the time and/or money constraints of an online service. At the current time, we are not charging users for optical media systems. The fixed costs of a subscription make budgeting somewhat easier, although the continuing appearance of new products and the length of our budget planning time line are in conflict. A disadvantage is with the frequency of updates. So far, our users have not minded this. They are still intrigued with the concept and the technology and have not yet reached the stage of criticism of fine points. It will be interesting to see what happens with pricing and contracts if more frequent updates and/or smooth interface to an online system for the latest update are clamored for by the market."

In the future, O'Neill Library is likely to add Medline, Chemical Abstracts, Biological Abstracts, INSPEC, or another product in the sciences next. It is also considering ways in which optically stored data (text and images) could be used with an expert system to teach manual and computerized research skills in library instruction programs.

UNIVERSITY LIBRARY
University of Nevada-Reno
Reno, Nevada

Type of library: Academic
Size of population served: 14,000
General description of user population: Undergraduate and graduate students, faculty, staff, community
Optical products in use: LaserQuest

The University Library picked LaserQuest in 1986 as an inexpensive method of doing retrospective data conversion. LaserQuest provides extraction and editing of full MARC records from a large resource database stored on discs; it also offers original cataloging of records and updating of a customer's MARC records, if they are stored in the GRC Resource database. Carol Parkhurst reports that "LaserQuest is being used in the UNR Library and at the Nevada State Library and the University of Las Vegas Library for retrospective conversion of serials records. The converted records will be loaded into the statewide Union List of Serials (in GRC) and will be used in our in-house automated systems.

"The LaserQuest station, which is an IBM PC with a Hitachi CDR-2500S drive, is located in the Catalog Department, and is used by bibliographic searching staff and data entry staff. Staff are trained by the Union List of Serials coordinator. The station is in use most of the day (8:00 a.m. to 5 p.m.). Serial records are searched in the CD-ROM database, then printed out in MARC format for review. Holdings statements are added to the printout, then keyed into

LaserQuest using a special 'serial holdings' screen. Records are downloaded to diskette and either transmitted over telephone lines or sent by mail to General Research Corporation to be loaded into the Nevada database. Edit lists are received every month. The records will be made available when needed to be tape loaded into our local online catalog." The Library converts between 150 and 200 serial titles per week, and has a 90 percent hit rate.

Among the system's advantages cited by Parkhurst are: (1) low cost for retrospective conversion; (2) ability to edit records as they are converted; (3) ease of use; (4) availability at all hours; (5) large size of database; and (6) lack of telecommunications costs. Parkhurst cites one disadvantage: Only one user at a time can utilize the system. Vendor documentation, which was initially poor, has been revised; telephone support is rated "excellent."

Appendix A
Producers and Distributors of Optical Information Products

The following list of companies involved in the production and distribution of optical media is divided into five sections according to type of product or service: (1) reference/information products; (2) cataloging and technical services products; (3) disc mastering, processing, and publishing systems; (4) retrieval software developers; and (5) hardware manufacturers. Only existing and marketed products and manufacturers have been listed; prototypes of products and those still in development are not included. Companies and products that do not have direct library application, such as those designed for industrial purposes, also are not included.

For more information about products and vendors, see Nancy Melin Nelson's *Library Applications of Optical Disk and CD-ROM Technology* (Meckler Publishing, 1987) as well as her *CD-ROMS in Print* (Meckler, 1987), and Bruce Connolly's "Laserdisk Directory" in each issue of *DATABASE* and *ONLINE* for 1986. Joe Ryan's column in *CD-ROM Librarian* and Janet M. Tiampo's column in *CD-ROM Review* provide updated listings of products and companies. Critical reviews of optical products can be found regularly in *CD-ROM Librarian*, *CD-ROM Review*, and *The Laserdisk Professional*.

REFERENCE/INFORMATION PRODUCTS

ALDE Publishing
4830 West 77th St.
P. O. Box 35326
Minneapolis, MN 55435
612-835-5240
Products: Pravda; Source 21: USSR;
  public domain software discs

American Library Association
50 East Huron St.
Chicago, IL 60611
312-944-6780; 800-545-2433
Product: Directory of Library and
  Information Professionals

Aries Systems Corp.
79 Boxford St.
North Andover, MA 01845
617-689-9334
Product: MEDLINE Knowledge
Finder

Auto-graphics, Inc.
3201 Temple Ave.
Pomona, CA 91768
800-325-7961; 714-595-7204
Product: IMPACT: Government
Documents database

R. R. Bowker
Electronic Publishing
245 West 17th St.
New York, NY 10011
800-323-3288
Products: Books in Print Plus;
Books in Print/Out of Print Plus;
Reviews Plus; Ulrich's Plus

Brodart Co.
Library Automation Division
500 Arch St.
Williamsport, PA 17705
800-233-8467 (ext. 640)
Product: Le Pac: Government
Documents Option

BRS Information Technologies
1200 Route 7
Latham, NY 12110
518-783-1161
Product: BRS/Colleague

Buckmaster Publishing
Route 3, Box 56
Mineral, VA 23117
800-282-5628; 703-894-5777
Product: Place Name Index

Cambridge Scientific Abstracts
720 Wisconsin Ave., N.W.
Bethesda, MD 20814
800-227-3052; 301-951-6750
Products: COMPACT Cambridge
series: Aquatic Sciences and
Fisheries Abstracts; Life Sciences
Collection; MEDLINE

Canadian Centre for Occupational
Health & Safety
250 Main St. East
Hamilton, ON Canada L8N 1H6
416-572-2981
Product: Ccinfodisc:

Chadwyck-Healey Inc.
Electronic Publishing Division
1101 King St.
Alexandria, VA 22314
703-683-4890; 800-752-0515
Product: Supermap (U.S. census
information and mapping)

Congressional Information Service
4520 East-West Hwy.
Suite 800
Bethesda, MD 20814
800-638-8380; 301-654-1550
Product: CIS Congressional
Masterfile 1789-1969

Data Base Products, Inc.
12770 Coit Rd., #1111
Dallas, TX 75251
214-233-0593; 800-345-2876
Product: O & D Plus Vol. 1-3 (U. S.
Dept. of Transportation's Origin
and Destination Survey for the
last 7 years)

Datatek
818 NW 63rd St.
Oklahoma City, OK 73116
405-843-7323
Product: DataTimes (The Daily
Oklahoman 1981-1986)

Dataware, Inc.
2 Greenwich Plaza
Suite 100
Greenwich, CT 06830
203-622-3908
Product: Happenstadt Directory of
Large Corporations

Datext, Inc.
444 Washington St.
Woburn, MA 01801
617-938-6667
Products: CD/Corporate; CD/Corp
Tech; CD/Newsline; CD/Banking;
CD/Private +; CD/International

DeLORME Mapping Systems
Lower Main St.
P. O. Box 298
Freeport, ME 04032
207-865-4171
Product: DeLORME's World Atlas

DIALOG Information Services
3460 Hillview Ave.
Palo Alto, CA 94304
800-334-2564; 415-858-3785
Products: DIALOG OnDisc: ERIC,
MEDLINE, AgriBusiness;
Canadian Business and Current
Affairs; Standard and Poor's
Corporations

Digital Diagnostics Inc.
1050 46th St.
Sacramento, CA 95819
916-456-5931; 800-826-5595
Product: BiblioMed

Disclosure, Inc.
5161 River Rd.
Bethesda, MD 20816
800-638-8076; 301-951-1300
Product: Compact Disclosure

EBSCO Publishing
P. O. Box 1943
Birmingham, AL 35201
800-826-3024; 205-991-1182
Products: Core MEDLINE;
Comprehensive MEDLINE; The
Serials Directory

*Educational Resources Information
Center (ERIC)*
ORI, Inc.
Information Systems Division
4833 Rugby Ave., Suite 301
Bethesda, MD 20814
301-656-9723

Product: ERIC through
SilverPlatter, DIALOG OnDisc,
OCLC

Ellis Enterprises Inc.
225 NW Thirteenth St.
Oklahoma City, OK 73103
405-235-7660
Products: The Bible Library; The
Nurse Library; The Physician
Library

Elsevier Science Publishing Co., Inc.
North American Database
Department
52 Vanderbilt Ave.
New York, NY 10017
212-916-1160
Product: EMBASE through
SilverPlatter

ERM Computer Services Inc.
999 West Chester Pike
West Chester, PA 19382
800-544-3118
Product: Enflex Info

Facts on File, Inc.
460 Park Ave. South
New York, NY 10016
212-683-2244
Product: Visual Dictionary
CD-ROM

GEOVISION Inc.
270 Scientific Dr., Suite 1
Norcross, GA 30092
404-448-8224
Product: GEOdisc

Grolier Electronic Publishing, Inc.
Sherman Turnpike
Danbury, CT 06816
800-356-5590
Product: Electronic Encyclopedia
(Academic American Encyclope-
dia)

Highlighted Data
P. O. Box 17229
Washington, DC 20041
703-533-1939
Products: Merriam-Webster Ninth
New Collegiate Dictionary;
Electronic Map Cabinet

Horizon Information Services
1900 South Sepulveda, Suite 220
Los Angeles, CA 90025
213-479-4966
Product: MEDLINE-CD

Information Access Co.
11 Davis Dr.
Belmont, CA 94002
800-227-8431; 415-591-2333
Products: InfoTrac; InfoTrac II;
Academic Index; Government
Publications Index; LegalTrac;
Wall Street Journal Database

Information Design Inc.
1300 Charleston Rd.
P. O. Box 7130
Mountain View, CA 94039
415-969-7990
Product: Zip + 4

Information Handling Services Inc.
2001 Jefferson Davis Highway,
Suite 1201
Arlington, VA 22202
703-521-5000; 800-241-7824
Product: Personnet

Institute for Scientific Information
3501 Market St.
Philadelphia, PA 19104
215-386-0100
Product: Science Citation Index on
CD-ROM

JA Micropublishing Inc.
271 Main St., Box 218
Westchester, NY 10707
914-793-2130; 800-227-2477
Product: CIRR

Knowledge Access International
2685 Marine Way, Suite 1305
Mountain View, CA 94043
415-969-0606
Products: Consumer Drug
Information On Disk; Your
Marketing Consultant: Business
to Business

Library Association
7 Ridgemount St.
London, WC1E 7AE United
Kingdom
01-36-7543
Product: LISA through SilverPlatter

Library Corporation
P. O. Box 40035
Washington, DC 20016
800-624-0559; 304-229-0100
Product: Any-book

Lotus Development Corp.
55 Cambridge Parkway
Cambridge, MA 02142
617-577-8500; 800-554-5501
Products: One Source; Computer
Library

McGraw-Hill Book Co.
1221 Avenue of the Americas, 48th
Floor
New York, NY 10020
212-512-2000; 800-262-4729
Products: McGraw-Hill CD-ROM
Science & Technical Reference
Set; Electronic Sweet's

Micromedex, Inc.
2750 South Shoshone St.
Englewood, CO 80110
800-525-9083
Products: Drugdex; Emergindex;
Indentindex; Poisindex

Microsoft
16011 NE 36th Way
Box 97017
Redmond, WA 98073-9717
206-882-8080; 800-426-9400
Products: Microsoft Bookshelf;
Small Business Consultant

MicroTrends, Inc.
650 Woodfield Drive, Suite 730
Schaumburg, IL 60195
312-310-8928
Products: BioLibe series; FastPast;
LinguaTech Bilingual Dictionaries; Nature Plus; Menu; Versa Text

Modern Language Association
10 Astor Place
New York, NY 10003
214-614-6350
Product: MLA International Bibliography on WILSONDISC

National Agricultural Library
1301 Baltimore Blvd.
Beltsville, MD 20705
301-344-3755
Products: Pork Producers' Handbook; Agricola

National Gallery of Art
Dept. of Extension Programs
4th Street and Constitution Avenue S.W.
Washington, DC 20565
202-842-6263
Product: National Gallery of Art Videodisc

National Information Center for Educational Media (NICEM) and Access Innovations, Inc.
P. O. Box 40130
Albuquerque, NM 87196
800-421-8711; 505-265-3591
Product: A-V Online through SilverPlatter

National Library of Medicine
National Institutes of Health
Bethesda, MD 20209
301-487-4612
Product: MEDLINE

NewsBank Inc.
58 Pine St.
New Canaan, CT 06840
800-243-7694; 203-966-1100
Product: NewsBank Electronic Index

Newsreel Access Systems Inc.
340 East 93rd St., Suite 19E
New York, NY 10128
212-996-3035
Products: NewsScan; CineScan; PhotoScan

OCLC, Inc.
6565 Frantz Rd.
Dublin, OH 43017
614-764-6063; 800-848-5878
Products: Search CD450: Agricola; EMIL; ERIC; NTIS; Environment Library

Online Research Systems, Inc.
2901 Broadway, Suite 154
New York, NY 10025
212-408-3311
Product: Compact Med-Base

Optical Media International
P. O. Box 2107
Aptos, CA 95001
408-662-1772
Product: Universe of Sound

PC-SIG
1030D East Duane Ave.
Sunnyvale, CA 94086
408-730-9291
Products: PC-SIG Library; Science Helper; CD/Biotech

PCI Inc.
80 Bloor St., West Suite 1100
Toronto, ON M5S 2V1
416-928-6733
Product: Resors (publications on remote sensing)

Pergamon Compact Solution
Athene House
66-73 Shoe Lane
London, England EC4P 4AB
Product: International Encyclopedia of Education

Psychological Abstracts Information
  Services
1400 North Uhle Street
Arlington, VA 22201
800-336-4980; 703-247-7829
Product: PsycLIT through
  SilverPlatter

Public Affairs Information Service,
  Inc.
11 W. 40th St.
New York, NY 10018-2693
212-736-6629; 800-841-2693
Product: PAIS on CD-ROM

Quantum Access Inc.
1700 W. Loop South, Suite 1460
Houston, TX 77027
713-622-3211
Products: The Texas State
  Education Encyclopedia; The
  Attorney General Documents

Reference Technology Inc.
5700 Flatiron Parkway
Boulder, CO 80301
800-225-2749; 303-449-4157
Products: Software Library
  DataPlate; CUSIP

SilverPlatter Information, Inc.
37 Walnut St.
Wellesley, MA 02181; 800-343-0064
617-239-0306; 800-343-0064
Products: A-V ONLINE; AGRIC-
  OLA; Business Software
  Database; Ca-CD; CHEM-BANK;
  CIRR; COMPU-INFO; EMBASE;
  ERIC; LISA; MEDLINE;
  Peterson's College Database;
  NTIS; OSH-ROM; PsycLIT;
  Sociofile

Slater Hall Information Products
1522 K St., N.W., Suite 1112
Washington, DC 20005
202-682-1350
Products: SHIP Discs (Business and
  population statistics); Census of
  Agriculture 1982

Sociological Abstracts
P. O. Box 22206
San Diego, CA 92122
619-565-6603
Product: Sociofile through
  SilverPlatter

Standard & Poor's Compustat
  Services, Inc.
7400 South Alton Court
Englewood, CO 80112
800-525-8640
Product: Compustat PC Plus on
  CD-ROM

Tescor Inc.
461 Carlisle Drive
Herndon, VA 22070
703-435-9501; 800-842-0077
Product: First National Item Bank
  & Test Development System

Thesaurus Linguae Graecae
University of California, Irvine
Irvine, CA 92717
714-856-6404
Product: TLG Databank of Ancient
  Greek Texts

Tri-Star Publishing
475 Virginia Drive
Fort Washington, PA 19034
215-641-6000
Products: Oxford English Dictionary; Trademark Information
  Database

University Microfilms International
  (UMI)
UMI Electronic Publishing
300 North Zeeb Rd.
Ann Arbor, MI 48106
800-732-0616; 313-761-4700 (ext.
  505)
Products: Dissertation Abstracts
  OnDisc; ABI-INFORM;
  Newspaper Abstracts

US West Knowledge Engineering
4380 S. Syracuse, Suite 600
Denver, CO 80237
303-694-4200; 800-222-0920
Product: Hydrodata

VLS Inc.
310 Reynolds Rd.
Toledo, OH 43625
419-536-5820
Product: OPTEXT (CFR and
   Federal Register)

Wiley Electronic Publishing
605 Third Ave.
New York, NY 10158
212-850-6331
Products: Registry of Mass Spectral
   Data; Kirk-Othmer Encyclopedia
   of Chemical Technology;
   International Dictionary of
   Medicine and Biology; Mark
   Encyclopedia of Polymer Science
   and Engineering

H. W. Wilson Company
950 University Ave.
Bronx, NY 10542
212-588-8400
Products: WILSONDISC series:
   Reader's Guide to Periodical
   Literature, Applied Science and
   Technology Index, Art Index,
   Social Sciences Index, Library
   Literature, Modern Language
   Association International
   Bibliography, Humanities Index,
   Business Periodicals Index,
   Biography Index, Index to Legal
   Periodicals, General Science
   Index, Cumulative Book Index,
   Education Index, GPO Monthly
   Catalog, Biological and
   Agricultural Index

CATALOGING AND TECHNICAL SERVICES PRODUCTS

Auto-graphics, Inc.
3201 Temple Ave.
Pomona, CA 91768
800-325-7961; 714-595-7204
Product: IMPACT

Baker & Taylor
50 Kirby Ave.
Somerville, NJ 08876
800-526-3811
Product: BaTaSystems

Blackwell North America Inc.
6024 SW Jean Rd.
Building G
Lake Oswego, OR 97084
Product: PC Order Plus

Brodart Co.
Library Automation Division
500 Arch St.
Williamsport, PA 17705
800-233-8467 (ext. 640)
Product: Le Pac: Local Public
   Access Catalogue

EBSCO Publishing
P. O. Box 1943
Birmingham, AL 35201
800-826-3024; 205-991-1182
Products: Cataloger's Tool Kit;
   Reference Tool Kit; EBSCO
   Serials Directory

Faxon Company
15 Southwest Park
Westwood, MA 02090
617-329-3350
Product: MicroLinx/CD-ROM
   Serial Service

General Research Corporation,
   Library Systems
P. O. Box 6770
Santa Barbara, CA 93160-6770
800-235-6788
Products: LaserGuide; LaserQuest

Ingram Book Company
347 Reedwood Dr.
Nashville, TN 37217
800-251-5902
Products: LaserSearch; Flash-Back

Library Corporation
P. O. Box 40035
Washington, DC 20016
800-624-0559; 304-229-0100
Products: BiblioFile; The Intelligent
Catalog

Library Systems and Services Inc.
(LSSI)
20251 Century Blvd.
Germantown, MD 20874
800-638-8725; 301-258-0200
Products: LaserFile; PC/MARC;
MINI MARC II

Marcive, Inc.
P. O. Box 47508
San Antonio, TX 78265
800-531-7678; 512-646-6161
Product: MARCIVE/PAC

OCLC, Inc.
6565 Frantz Rd.
Dublin, OH 43017-0702
614-764-6000; 800-848-5878
Product: CD Cataloging System

Sirsi Corporation
8106 South Memorial Parkway
Huntsville, AL 35802
205-881-2140
Product: Lasertap

Small Library Computing Inc.
48 Lawrence Ave.
Holbrook, NY 11741
516-588-1387
Products: Bib-Base/CD-ROM;
Ultracard/CD-ROM

Sydney Dataproducts, Inc.
11075 Santa Monica Blvd., Suite
100
Los Angeles, CA 90025
800-992-9778; 213-479-4621
Product: CD-ROM cataloging
system

UTLAS International
1611 North Kent St., Suite 910
Arlington, VA 22209
800-368-3008
Products: DisCat; DisCon; UTLAS
Spectrum M/100

Western Library Network (WLN)
Washington State University
Mail Stop AJ-11W
Olympia, WA 98504
206-459-6518
Product: LaserCat

DISC MASTERING, PROCESSING, AND PUBLISHING SYSTEMS

AMTEC Information Services, Inc.
3700 Industry Ave.
Lakewood, CA 90714-6050
213-595-4756
Service: page imaging and digitizing

CD-ROM Publishing Service Inc.
212 King St. West, #202
Toronto, ON Canada M5H 1K5
419-591-1707
Service: CD-ROM publishing

Database Development
Marine Plaza, Suite 1224
111 E. Wisconsin Ave.
Milwaukee, WI 53202
414-765-0203
Services: product design and
development

Database Services, Inc.
2685 Marine Way, Suite 1305
Mountain View, CA 94043
415-961-2880
Services: product development and
marketing

Digital Audio Disk Corp.
1800 N. Fruitridge Ave.
Terre Haute, IN 47805
812-466-6821
Service: CD-ROM disc replication

Discovery Systems
555 Metro Place North
Columbus, OH 43107
614-761-2000
Service: CD-ROM disc replication

Information Workstation Group
501 Queen St.
Alexandria, VA 22314
703-548-4320
Services: CD-ROM and WORM
  publishing

International Development Center
3514 Plyers Mill Rd.
Kensington, MD 20895
301-949-0220
Service: data conversion

International Software Database
1520 South College Ave.
Fort Collins, CO 80524
800-The-Menu; 303-482-5000
Service: WORM development

Laser Magnetic Storage
International Co.
4425 Arrows West Drive
Colorado Springs, CO 80907
303-593-4269
Service: CD-ROM publishing

LaserData, Inc.
10 Technology Dr.
Lowell, MA 01851
617-937-5900
Service: page imaging

Meridian Data, Inc.
4450 Capitola Rd., Suite 101
Capitola, CA 95010
408-476-5858
Products: In-house CD-ROM
  publishing system; CD-Net
  networking system

Offshore Information Services
39 North Broadway
Tarrytown, NY 10591
914-631-1757
Service: data conversion

Optical Media International
485 Alberto Way
Los Gatos, CA 95030
408-395-4332
Product: In-house CD-ROM
  publishing system

Optimage Interactive Services Co.
300 West Adams St., Suite 601
Chicago, IL 60606
312-782-8229
Services: CD-ROM design and
  premastering

Philips and DuPont Optical Co.
1409 Foulk Rd., Suite 2000
Wilmington, DE 19803
302-479-2500
Services: CD-ROM premastering,
  mastering, and replication

Publishers Data Service Corporation
2511 Garden Rd., Bldg. C
Monterey, CA 93940
408-372-2812
Service: Data preparation and
  scanning

Riley and Johnson
1990 M Street, N. W., Suite 400
Washington, DC 20036
202-362-6662
Service: CD-ROM system design

Saztec International
27520 Hawthorne Blvd., #170
Rolling Hills Estate, CA 90274
213-544-0337
Service: CD-ROM disc mastering

3M Optical Recording Project
3M Center, Bldg. 225-4S-09
St. Paul, MN 55144
612-736-9581
Service: CD-ROM disc replication

RETRIEVAL SOFTWARE DEVELOPERS

Access Innovations, Inc.
P. O. Box 40130-4314
Albuquerque, NM 87196
800-421-8711; 505-265-3591
Product: Retrieval software for
AV-ONLINE

Borland International
4585 Scotts Valley Dr.
Scotts Valley, CA 95066
408-438-8400
Product: PARADOX

Computer Access Corporation
26 Brighton St., Suite 324
Belmont, MA 02178-4008
617-484-2412
Product: BlueFish

Del Mar Group, Inc.
722 Genevieve, Suite M
Solana Beach, CA 92075
619-259-0444
Product: SmarTrieve

Digital Equipment Corp.
CD Publishing Group
12 Crosby Dr.
Bedford, MA 01730
617-276-1345
Product: VAX VTX

Fulcrum Technologies Inc.
560 Rochester St., 3rd Floor
Ottawa, ON Canada K1S 5K2
613-238-1761
Product: FULCRUM Ful/Text

Group L Corporation
481 Carlisle Drive
Herndon, VA 22070
703-471-0030
Product: DELVE

Information Dimensions, Inc.
655 Metro Place South
Dublin, OH 43017-1396
614-761-7300; 800-328-2648
Product: MicroBASIS

Knowledge Access International
2685 Marine Way, Suite 1305
Mountain View, CA 94043
415-969-0606
Product: KAware

KnowledgeSet Corp.
2511C Garden Road
Monterey, CA 93940
408-375-2638
Product: KRS (Knowledge Retrieval
System)

Online Computer Systems, Inc.
20251 Century Blvd.
Germantown, MD 20874
800-922-9204
Product: various applications
software

Personal Library Software
15215 Shady Grove Rd., Suite 204
Rockville, MD 20850
301-926-1402
Product: Personal Librarian

Reference Technology, Inc.
1832 N. 55th St.
Boulder, CO 80301
303-449-4157
Product: Full Text Manager; Key
Record Manager

Reteaco, Inc.
1051 Clinton St.
Buffalo, NY 14206
800-387-5002
Product; FindIT

TMS, Inc.
7840 Computer Ave.
Minneapolis, MN 55435
612-835-4399
Products: TMS RESEARCH; Disc
Architecture Software

HARDWARE MANUFACTURERS

Amdek Corp.
1901 Zanker Rd.
San Jose, CA 95112
408-436-8570

Apple Computer Inc.
20525 Mariani Ave.
Cupertino, CA 95014
408-973-6144

Denon
222 New Rd.
Parsippany, NJ 07054
201-575-7810

Digital Equipment Corp.
2 Mount Royal Ave.
Marlboro, MA 01752
800-258-1710

*Hitachi Sales Corporation of
America*
401 West Artesia Blvd.
Compton, CA 90020
213-537-8383

JVC
41 Slater Drive
Elmwood Park, NJ 07407
201-794-3900

KnowledgeSet Corp.
2511C Garden Rd.
Monterey, CA 93940
408-375-2638

Laser Magnetic Storage
4425 ArrowsWest Dr.
Colorado Springs, CO 80907
303-593-4269; 303-593-4270

Panasonic
1 Panasonic Way
Secaucus, NJ 07094
201-392-4602

Phillips Subsystems and Peripherals
100 East 42nd Street
New York, NY 10017
212-850-5011

Reference Technology, Inc.
5700 Flatiron Parkway
Boulder, CO 80301
303-449-4157

Sanyo
51 Joseph St.
Moonachie, NJ 07074
201-440-9300

Sony Corporation
1 Sony Drive
Park Ridge, NJ 07656
201-930-6104

Toshiba America, Inc.
Disk Products Division
3910 Freedom Circle, #103
Santa Clara, CA 95054
408-727-3939

Appendix B
Optical Information Systems:
A Selective Bibliography

Current literature concerning the development, uses and implications of optical technology generally falls into the following nine categories: (1) bibliographies, (2) basic texts, (3) directories and guides, (4) technical discussions, (5) standardization discussions, (6) general discussions, (7) reference and public service applications, (8) technical services applications, and (9) other applications. In the following selective bibliography, representative titles from each category are included, limited to those materials published between January 1985 and May 1988. Also included here is a list of currently published periodicals that deal primarily with optical information. For references to articles published before 1984, see the comprehensive bibliography at the end of C. M. Goldstein's "Computer-based Information Storage Technologies" in *Annual Review of Information Science and Technology* (v. 19, 1984, pp. 65–96).

To keep up-to-date with new products and applications, check Nancy Herther's column, "The Silver Disk," appearing in each issue of both *ONLINE* and *DATABASE*, as well as Julie Schwerin's column, "Optical Publishing," appearing monthly in *Information Today*. Critical reviews of individual optical products can be found in each issue of *CD-ROM Librarian*, *CDROM Review*, and *The Laserdisk Professional*.

BIBLIOGRAPHIES

Compact Optical Disc Technology—CD ROM, April 1979–1986: Citations from the INSPEC Database. Springfield, VA: National Technical Information Service, 1986. PB87-852885/XAB.

Optical Memory Data Storage, 1975–February 1986: Citations from the INSPEC Database. Springfield, VA: National Technical Information Service, 1986. PB86-858248/XAB.

Rechel, Michael W. "Laser Disc Technology: A Selective Introductory Bibliography." *CD-ROM Librarian* 2 (4) (July/August 1987): 16–24.

———. "How to Keep Up: Absolutely Essential CD-ROM Reading." *Wilson Library Bulletin* 62 (4) (December 1987): 41–42.

Timbers, Jill G. "Laserdisc Technology: A Review of the Literature on Videodisc and Optical Disc Technology, 1983–mid-1985." *Library Hi Tech Bibliography* 1 (1986): 57–66.

BASIC TEXTS

Council on Library Resources. *Videodisc and Optical Digital Disk Technologies and Their Applications in Libraries.* Washington, DC: Council on Library Resources, 1985.

Hendley, Tony. *CD-ROM and Optical Publishing Systems.* Westport, CT: Meckler Publishing Corp., 1987.

———. *Videodiscs, Compact Disks and Digital Optical Disk Systems.* Medford, NJ: Learned Information, 1986.

Isailovic, Jordan. *Videodisc Systems: Theory and Applications.* Englewood Cliffs, NJ: Prentice-Hall, 1987.

Lambert, Steve, and Ropiequet, Suzanne, eds. *The New Papyrus, CD-ROM.* Bellevue, WA: Microsoft Press, 1986.

McQueen, Judy, and Boss, Richard W. *Videodisk and Optical Digital Disk Technologies and Their Applications in Libraries, 1986 Update.* Chicago: American Library Association, 1986.
This is an update of the Council on Library Resources volume cited above.

Ropiequet, Suzanne, ed. *CD-ROM 2: Optical Publishing.* Bellevue, WA: Microsoft Press, 1987.

Saffady, William. *Optical Disks for Data and Document Storage.* Westport, CT: Meckler Publishing, 1986.

———. *Optical Storage Technology 1987: A State of the Art Review.* Westport, CT: Meckler Publishing, 1987.

DIRECTORIES AND GUIDES

AIIM Buying Guide: The Official Registry of Information and Image Management Products and Services. Silver Spring, MD: Association for Information and Image Management, 1985–.

Bowers, Richard A. *Optical Publishing Directory, 1987.* Medford, NJ: Learned Information, 1987.

Buddine, Laura, and Young, Elizabeth. *Brady Guide to CD-ROM.* New York, NY: Prentice-Hall, 1987.

Connolly, Bruce. "Laserdisk Directory—Part 1." *DATABASE* 9 (3) (June 1986): 15–26.

———. "Laserdisk Directory—Part 2." *ONLINE* 10 (4) (July 1986): 39–49.

———. "Laserdisk Directory—Part 3." *DATABASE* 9 (4) (August 1986): 34–39.

———. "Laserdisk Directory—Part 4." *ONLINE* 10 (5) (September 1986): 54–58.

———. "Laserdisk Directory—Part 5." *DATABASE* 9 (6) (December 1986): 46–48.

"Directory of WORM (Write-once, Read-many) Companies and Organizations." *Optical Information Systems* 7 (3) (May/June 1987): 185–92.

Gale, John. *State of the CD-ROM Industry: Applications, Players, and Products.* Alexandria, VA: Information Workstation Group, 1987– .
This is a two-volume subscription service, updated quarterly.

Gale, John, Lynch, Clifford, and Brownrigg, Edward. *Report on CD-ROM Search Software.* Alexandria, VA: Information Workstation Group, 1987.

Helgerson, Linda, and Ennis, Martin. *The CD-ROM Sourcebook.* Falls Church, VA: Diversified Data Resources, 1986.

Nelson, Nancy Melin. *CD-ROMS in Print.* Westport, CT: Meckler, 1987– .

———. *Library Applications of Optical Disk and CD-ROM Technology. (Essential Guide to the Library IBM PC, vol. 8.)* Westport, CT: Meckler Publishing, 1986.

Roth, Judith Paris, ed. *Essential Guide to CD-ROM.* Westport, CT: Meckler Publishing, 1986.

Saffady, William. *Video-based Information Systems: A Guide for Educational, Business, Library, and Home Use.* Chicago: American Library Association, 1985.

"Videodisc Projects Directory." *Optical Information Systems* 7 (1) (January/February 1987): 74–77.

Who's Who in Optical Memories and Interactive Videodisks. San Francisco, CA: Rothchild Consultants, 1983– .

RETRIEVAL SOFTWARE ISSUES AND OTHER TECHNICAL DISCUSSIONS

Byers, T. J. "Built by Association." *PC World* 5 (4) (April 1987): 245–251.

Chen, Peter Pin-Shan. "The Compact Disk ROM: How It Works." *IEEE Spectrum* 23 (4) (April 1986): 44–49.

Dulude, Jeffrey R. "The Application Interface of Optical Drives." *BYTE* 11 (5) (May 1986): 193–199.

Free, John. "The Laser-disc Revolution." *Popular Science* 229 (5) (May 1985): 66–68, 107–110.

Gussin, Larry Dane. "Hypertext: From the Lab to the Workplace." *CD-ROM Review* 3 (3) (May 1988): 24.

Helgerson, Linda W. "CD-ROM Search and Retrieval Software: The Requirements and Realities." *Library Hi Tech* 4 (2) (Summer 1986): 69–77.

Herther, Nancy. "Access Software for Optical/Laser Information Packages." *DATABASE* 9 (4) (August 1986): 93–97.

——. "Text Retrieval Software for Microcomputers." *DATABASE* 9 (6) (November 1986): 125–129.

Moes, Robert J. "The CD-ROM Puzzle: Where Do the Pieces Fit?" *Optical Information Systems* 6 (6) (November/December 1986): 509–511.

Myers, Patti. *Publishing with CD-ROM: A Guide to Compact Disc Optical Storage Technologies for Providers of Publishing Services.* Westport, CT: Meckler Publishing, 1986.

"Optical Disk Technology." Special Section in *Bulletin of the American Society for Information Science* 13 (6) (August/September 1987): 11–29.
Includes a series of articles concerning optical publishing standards, using videodiscs for training, current trends and future predictions for optical technologies, among others.

Oren, Tim, and Kildall, Gary A. "The Compact Disk ROM: Applications Software." *IEEE Spectrum* 23 (4) (April 1986): 49–54.

Rivett, Mike. "Videodiscs and Digital Optical Disks." *Journal of Information Science: Principles and Practices* 13 (1) (1987): 25–34.

Smith, Karen E. "Hypertext—Linking to the Future." *ONLINE* 12 (2) (March 1988): 32–40.

"Theme: Mass Storage." *BYTE* 11 (5) (May 1986): 159– 246.
This special section on laser-based technology is composed of seven different articles dealing with technical issues. Of particular interest are Leonard Laub's "The Evolution of Mass Storage" (pp. 161–72), Norman Desmarais's "Laser Libraries" (pp. 235–46), and Bill Zoellick's "CD-ROM Software Development" (pp. 177–88).

Tiampo, Janet M. "Data Retrieval: The Search Is On." *CD-ROM Review* 2 (3) (May/June 1987): 27–31.
————. "A View of Something New." *CD-ROM Review* 3 (3) (May 1988): 46–47.

STANDARDIZATION DISCUSSIONS

Desmarais, Norman. "The Status of CD-ROM Standards." *CD-ROM Librarian* 2 (4) (July/August 1987): 11–15.
Harris, Patricia. "NISO CD-ROM Standards Update." *CD-ROM Librarian* 3 (1) (January 1988): 8–9.
Lynch, Clifford A. "Standards Issues for Optical Publishing." *Bulletin of the American Society for Information Science* 13 (6) (August/September 1987): 27–29.
Schwerin, Julie. *CD-ROM Standards: The Book.* Medford, NJ: Learned Information, 1986.

GENERAL DISCUSSIONS

"AL Automation Symposium: Will Optical Discs Be the End of Online Networks?" *American Libraries* 18 (4) (April 1987): 253–256.
Alberico, Ralph. "Justifying CD-ROM." *Small Computers in Libraries* 7 (2) (February 1987): 18–20.
Artlip, P. M. "How to Choose the Right Media: Optical, Magnetic, or Microfilm?" *Journal of Information and Image Management* 18 (9) (September 1985): 14–17.
Bairstow, Jeffrey. "CD-ROM Mass Storage for the Mass Market." *High Technology* 6 (10) (October 1986): 44–51.
Banks, R. L. "COM vs. Optical Disks: Where's the Beef?" *Journal of Information and Image Management* 19 (2) (February 1986): 21–23, 30.
————. "COM vs. Optical Disks: Which Way to the Future?" *Information Management* 18 (4) (April 1985): 10–15.
Becker, Karen A. "CD-ROM: A Primer." *College & Research Libraries News* 48 (7) (July/August 1987): 388–393.
CD ROM: Revolution Maker. The COINT Reports (vol. 6, no. 5). Morton Grove, IL: Info Digest, 1986.
"CD ROM Special Report." *PC World* 5 (4) (April 1987): 220–259.
This special report consists of seven discussions of different aspects of the present state and future promise of CD-ROM, CD-I, and other optical technologies.

"CD-ROM vs Online: Can Both Exist?" Special section in *Bulletin of the American Society for Information Science* 14 (1) (October/November 1987): 14–27.
A special section of nine articles discussing the future of online in the face of increasing use of CD-ROM.

Chen, Ching-chih. "Micro-based Optical Videodisc Applications." *Microcomputers for Information Management* 2 (4) (December 1985): 217–40.

Cohen, Elaine, and Young, Margo. "Cost Comparison of Abstracts and Indexes on Paper, CD-ROM, and Online." *Optical Information Systems* 6 (6) (November/December 1986): 485–490.

Connolly, Bruce. "Looking Backward—CDROM and the Academic Library of the Future." *ONLINE* 11 (3) (May 1987): 56-59.

Crane, Nancy, and Durfee, Tamara. "Entering Uncharted Territory: Putting CD-ROM in Place." *Wilson Library Bulletin* 62 (4) (December 1987): 28–30.

Eaton, Nancy L., and Crane, Nancy B. "Integrating Electronic Information Systems into the Reference Services Budget." *The Reference Librarian* 19 (1987): 161–177.

Helgerson, Linda W. "CD-ROM: A Revolution in the Making." *Library Hi Tech* 4 (1) (Spring 1986): 23–27.

Henderson, Earl, and Thoma, George. "Optical Technology: Impact on Information Transfer." *The Bowker Annual of Library & Book Trade Information,* 30th ed., pp. 91–102. New York: R. R. Bowker Co., 1985.

Herther, Nancy. "Access to Information: An Optical Disk Solution." *Wilson Library Bulletin* 60 (9) (May 1986): 19–21.

———. "CDROM and Information Dissemination: An Update." *ONLINE* 11 (2) (March 1987): 56–64.

———. "CDROM Technology: A New Era for Information Storage and Retrieval?" *ONLINE* 9 (6) (November 1985): 17–28.

———. "A Planning Model for Optical Product Evaluation." *ONLINE* 10 (5) (September 1986): 128–30.

Jeffries, Ron. "Goodbye, Gutenberg!" *PC Magazine* 23 (4) (November 12, 1985): 95–98.

McManus, Reed. "CD ROM: The Little Leviathan." *PC World* 4 (10) (October 1986): 272–280.

Marmion, Dan. "Installing CD-ROM Systems: How Do We Do It?" *CD-ROM Librarian* 2 (6) (November/December 1987): 16-20.

Mendrinos, Roxanne Baxter. "CD-ROM: Research Strategies for a Lifetime." *Media & Methods* 23 (4) (March/April 1987): 8–11.

Miller, David C. "Evaluating CDROMS: To Buy or What to Buy?" *DATABASE* 10 (3) (June 1987): 36–42.

———. *The New Optical Media in the Library and the Academy To-morrow: A Special Report to the Fred Meyer Charitable Trust.* Portland, OR: Hypermap, January 1987.

———. *Publishers, Libraries, & CD-ROM: Implications of Digital Op-tical Printing. Special Report.* Portland, OR: DCM Associates, 1987.

Miller, Tim. "Early User Reaction to CD-ROM and Videodisc-Based Optical Information Products in the Library Market." *Optical Information Systems* 7 (3) (May/June 1987): 205–209.

Nelson, Nancy Melin. "The CD-ROM Industry: A Library Market Overview." *Wilson Library Bulletin* 62 (4) (December 1987): 19–20.

Optical Discs for Storage and Access in ARL Libraries. ARL SPEC Kit #133. Washington, DC: Systems and Procedures Exchange Center, 1987.

Optical Disk Technology at OCLC. (VHS videocassette) Prod. OCLC Video Communications Program. OCLC, 1986. 23 min. OCLC #13196641.

Paisley, William, and Butler, Matilda. "The First Wave: CD-ROM Adoption in Offices and Libraries." *Microcomputers for Informa-tion Management* 4 (2) (June 1987): 109–127.

Pooley, Christopher. "The CD-ROM Marketplace: A Producer's Per-spective." *Wilson Library Bulletin* 62 (4) (December 1987): 24–26.

Saviers, Shannon Smith. "Reflections on CD-ROM: Bridging the Gap Between Technology and Purpose." *Special Libraries* 78 (4) (Fall 1987): 288–94.

Schwerin, Julie B. "Optical Systems for Information Delivery and Storage." *Electronic Publishing Review* 5 (3) (September 1985): 193–198.

Slonin, Jacob, et al. "Write-once Laser Disc Technology." *Library Hi Tech* 3 (4) (Winter 1985): 27–42.

Stewart, Linda, and Olsen, Jan. "Compact Disk Databases: Are They Good For Users?" *ONLINE* 12 (3) (May 1988): 48–52.

Strauss, Diane. "A Checklist of Issues to Be Considered Regarding the Addition of Microcomputer Data Disks to Academic Librar-ies." *Information Technology and Libraries* 5 (2) (June 1986): 129–32.

Suprenant, Tom. "Future Libraries." *Wilson Library Bulletin* 61 (5) (January 1987): 52–53.

Tenopir, Carol. "Costs and Benefits of CD-ROM." *Library Journal* 112 (14) (September 1, 1987): 156–157.

Watson, Paula D. "Costs to Libraries of the Optical Information Rev-olution." *ONLINE* 12 (1) (January 1988): 45–50.

Waurzyniak, Patrick. "Optical Discs." *InfoWorld* 8 (49) (December 8, 1986): 51–55.

Williams, James B. *Optical Publishing and Higher Education: The Promise, The Risks, The Issues: A Special Report to Fred Meyer Charitable Trust.* Benecia, CA: DCM Associates, August 1986.

REFERENCE AND PUBLIC SERVICE APPLICATIONS

Abbott, G. L. "Video-based Information Systems in Academic Library Media Centers." *Library Trends* 34 (1) (Summer 1985): 151–159.

Beltran, Ann Bristow. "InfoTrac at Indiana University: A Second Look." *DATABASE* 10 (1) (February 1987): 48–50.

———. "Use of InfoTrac in a University Library." *DATABASE* 9 (3) (June 1986): 63–66.

Carney, Richard D. "InfoTrac vs. the Confounding of Technology and Its Applications." *DATABASE* 9 (3) (June 1986): 56–61.

Case, Donald Owen, and Welden, Kathleen. "Distribution of Government Publications to Depository Libraries by Optical Disk: A Review of the Technology, Applications and Issues." *Government Publications Review* 13 (3) (May/June 1986): 313–322.

Ernest, Douglas J., and Monath, Jennifer. "User Reaction to a Computerized Periodical Index." *College & Research Libraries News* 47 (5) (May 1986): 315–18.

Glitz, Beryl. "Testing the New Technology: MEDLINE on CD-ROM in an Academic Health Sciences Library." *Special Libraries* 79 (1) (Winter 1988): 28–33.

Graves, Gail T., Harper, Laura G., and King, Beth F. "Planning for CD-ROM in the Reference Department." *College & Research Libraries News* 48 (7) (July/August 1987): 393–400.

Hagan, Dalia. "The Tacoma Debut of *Books in Print Plus.*" *Library Journal* 112 (4) (September 1, 1987): 149–151.

Hall, Cynthia, et al. "InfoTrac in Academic Libraries: What's Missing in the New Technology?" *DATABASE* 10 (1) (February 1987): 52–56.

Jackson, Kathy M., King, Evelyn M., and Kellough, Jean. "How to Organize an Extensive Laserdisk Installation: The Texas A & M Experience." *ONLINE* 12 (2) (March 1988): 51–60.

Kleiner, Jane P. "InfoTrac: An Evaluation of System Use and Potential in Research Libraries." *RQ* 27 (2) (Winter 1987): 252–263.

Planning for End-User Searching: A Checklist of Questions. Prepared by the RASD MARS Direct Patron Access to Computer-based Reference Systems Committee of the American Library Association. *RASD MARS Occasional Papers*, no. 1, 1987.

Sabelhaus, Linda. "CD-ROM Use in an Association Special Library: A Case Study." *Special Libraries* 79 (2) (Spring 1988): 148–151.

Silver, Howard. "Managing a CD-ROM Installation: A Case Study at Hahnemann University." *ONLINE* 12 (2) (March 1988): 61–66.

Stewart, Linda. "Picking CD-Roms for Public Use." *American Libraries* 18 (9) (October 1987): 738–740.

Tucker, Sandra L., Anders, Vicki, and Clark, Katharine E., et al. "How to Manage an Extensive Laserdisk Installation: The Texas A & M Experience." *ONLINE* 12 (3) (May 1988): 34–46.

TECHNICAL SERVICES APPLICATIONS

Campbell, Brian. "Whither the White Knight: CD-ROM in Technical Services." *DATABASE* 10 (4) (August 1987): 22–40.

Desmarais, Norman. "Laserbases for Library Technical Services." *Optical Information Systems* 7 (1) (January/February 1987): 57–61.

Freund, A. L. "A Regional Bibliographic Database on Videodisc." *Library Hi Tech* 3 (2) (Summer 1985): 7–9.

Gatten, Jeffrey N., Ohles, Judy, and Gaylord, Mary Ardeth. "Purchasing CD-ROM Products: Considerations for a New Technology." *Library Acquisitions: Principles and Practices* 11 (4) (1987): 273–81.

Helgerson, Linda W. "Acquiring a CD-ROM Public Access Catalog System." *Library Hi Tech* 5 (3) (Fall 1987): 49–75.

Urbanski, Verna. "Resources and Technical Services News: CD-ROM Takes Center Stage." *Library Resources and Technical Services* 32 (1) (January 1988): 12–16.

Watson, Paula D., and Golden, Gary A. "Distributing an Online Catalog on CDROM." *ONLINE* 11 (2) (March 1987): 65–74.

OTHER APPLICATIONS

Allen, Marie. "Optical Character Recognition: Technology with New Relevance for Archival Automation Projects." *American Archivist* 50 (Winter 1987): 88–99.

Andre, Pamela Q. J. "Evaluating Laser Videodisc Technology for the Dissemination of Agricultural Information." *Information Technology and Libraries* 4 (2) (June 1985): 139–147.

————. "Full-text Access and Laser Videodiscs: The National Agricultural Library System." *Library Hi Tech* 4 (1) (Spring 1986): 13–21.

Bowles, Garrett H. "The Future of Music Databases." *Fontes Artis Musicae* 34 (1) (January 1987): 61–66.

Brewer, Bryan. "CD-ROM and CD-I." *CD-ROM Review* 2 (2) (May/June 1987): 18–25.

Brown, Jonathan R. "DATEXT—Using Business Information on CDROM." *ONLINE* 10 (5) (September 1986): 28–40.

Bruno, R., and Mizushima, M. "New Developments in Optical Media: An Outline of CD-I." *Optical Informations Systems* 6 (4) (July/August 1986): 318–23.

Cash, Joan. "Spinning Toward the Future: The Museum on Laser Videodisc." *Museum News* 63 (6) (August 1985): 19–35.

Crowley, Mary Jo. "Optical Digital Disk Storage: An Application for New Libraries." *Special Libraries* 79 (1) (Winter 1988): 34–42.

Davis, Douglas L. "Optical Archiving: Where Are We Now and Where Do We Go from Here?" *Optical Information Systems* 7 (1) (January/February 1987): 66–71.

Dubreuil, Lorraine. "Map Libraries and Optical Disks." *INSPEL* 21 (2) (1987): 97–100.

Hammond, Nancy. "Getting Started with Interactive Video." *Audiovisual Librarian* 13 (1) (February 1987): 38–45.

Helsel, Sandra Kay. "The Curricular Domain of Educational Interactive Videodisc." *Optical Information Systems* 7 (2) (March/April 1987): 107–12.

Irving, Ginny. "The Use of Optical Disks in Law Libraries." *Legal Reference Services Quarterly* 6 (2) (Spring/Summer 1986): 33–45.

Jones, Mark K. "Interactive Videodisc and the Self-Directed Learner." *Optical Information Systems* 7 (1) (January/February 1987): 62–65.

Lambert, Steve, and Sallis, Jane, eds. *CDI and Interactive Videodisc Technology.* Indianapolis, IN: Howard W. Sams, 1987.

Meadows, Laura Lou. "Training Students to Object." *PC Magazine* (April 16, 1985): 250–51.

Milan, Michael. "Interactive Videodisc at the National Computing Centre." *Audiovisual Librarian* 11 (1) (Winter 1985): 21–25.

Newman, Donald J. "Optical Disk and Micrographic Document Management Systems: Pros, Cons, and Draws." *Journal of Information and Image Management* 19 (9) (September 1986): 14–17.

Parker, Elisabeth Betz. "The Library of Congress Non Print Optical Disk Pilot Program." *Information Technology and Libraries* 4 (4) (December 1985): 289–99.

Price, J. W. "Optical Disks and Demand Printing Research at the Library of Congress." *Information Services and Use* 5 (1) (February 1985): 3–20.

"Records Management '86: The Year of the Optical Disk." Special section in *Modern Office Technology* 31 (1) (January 1986): 118–130.

Rowinsky, Walter. "Videodisks: Traditional Training Gets a New Twist." *PC Week* 2 (26) (July 2, 1985): 37–45.

Ryland, Jane N. "Storing Outer Space Data on Laser Disc." *Library Hi Tech* 3 (4) (Winter 1985): 77–79.

Stone, Claudia. "Next Stop: Compact Disc Interactive." *Publishers Weekly* 230 (July 4, 1986): 41–42.

PERIODICAL TITLES

Prices for the following publications are subject to change.

CD Data Report. 1984– . Monthly. $225. Langley Publications (1350 Beverly Rd., Suite 115-324, McLean, VA 22102, tel. 703-241-2131). Linda W. Helgerson, ed.

CD-ROM Librarian (formerly *Optical Information Systems Update: Library and Information Center Applications*) 1987– . 10/yr. $65. Meckler Publishing (11 Ferry Lane West, Westport, CT 06880, tel. 203-226-6967). Nancy Melin Nelson, ed.

CD-ROM Review. 1986– . Monthly. $34.97. CW Communications Inc. (80 Elm St., Peterborough, NH 03458, tel. 603-924-9471). Roger Strukhoff, ed.

DATABASE. 1975– . Bimonthly. $85. Online, Inc. (11 Tannery Lane, Weston, CT 06883, tel. 203-227-8466). Nancy Garman, ed.

Electronic and Optical Publishing Review. 1981– . Quarterly. $75. Learned Information (143 Old Marlton Pike, Medford, NJ 08055, tel. 609-654-6266). Julie B. Schwerin, ed.

Electronic Information Report. 1979– . $295. Link Resources Corp. (c/o International Data Corp., 79 Fifth Ave., New York, NY 10003, tel. 212-627-1400). Margaret T. Fischer, ed.

Electronic Publishing Business. 1983– . Monthly (except August). $95. Electronic Publishing Ventures (885 N. San Antonio Rd., Los Altos, CA 94022). Brian Aveney, ed.

Inform. (formerly *Journal of Information and Image Management*) 1987– . Monthly. $55. Association for Information and Image Management (1100 Wayne Ave., Suite 1100, Silver Spring, MD 20910, tel. 301-587-8202). Steve Fluty, ed.

Information Today. 1983– . 11/yr. $27.50. Learned Information (143 Old Marlton Pike, Medford, NJ 08055, tel. 609-654-6266). Bev Smith, ed.

The Laserdisk Professional. 1988– . Bimonthly. $85. Online, Inc. (11 Tannery Lane, Weston, CT 16883, tel. 302-227-8466.) Nancy K. Herther, ed.

Library Hi Tech. 1983– . Quarterly. $25. Pierian Press (Box 1808, Ann Arbor, MI 48106, tel. 313-434-6409). C. Edward Wall, ed.

ONLINE. 1977– . Bimonthly. $85. Online, Inc. (11 Tannery Lane, Weston, CT 16883, tel. 302-227-8466). Helen A. Gordon, ed.

Optical Information Systems (formerly *Videodisc and Optical Disk* and *Videodisc/Videotex*). 1981– . Bimonthly. $95. Meckler Publishing (11 Ferry Lane West, Westport, CT 06880, tel. 203-226-6967). Judith Paris Roth, ed.

Optical Information Systems Update (formerly *Videodisc and Optical Disk Update*). 1986– . 22/yr. $227. Meckler Publishing (11 Ferry Lane West, Westport, CT 06880, tel. 203-226-6967). Judith Paris Roth, ed.

Optical Memory News. 1983– . Bimonthly. $295. Rothchild Consultants (256 Laguna Honda Blvd., San Francisco, CA 94116, tel. 415-681-3700). Les Cowan, ed.

Videodisc Monitor. 1983– . Monthly. $247. Future Systems, Inc. (Box 26, Falls Church, VA 22046, tel. 703-241-1799). Rockley L. Miller, ed.

Index

Compiled by Linda Webster

Page numbers in italics indicate figures.

152   CD-ROM and Other Optical Information Systems

Nancy L. Eaton is director of libraries and media services, the University of Vermont and State Agricultural College, Burlington, VT. Under a cooperative agreement with the National Agricultural Library (NAL), she is National Project Manager for the National Agricultural Text Digitizing Project, a cooperative project between the NAL and 43 land grant libraries. She is a former president of the Library and Information Technology Association (LITA), a division of the American Library Association.

Linda Brew MacDonald is online services coordinator in the reference department at the Bailey/Howe Library at the University of Vermont, Burlington, VT, where she administers the mediated search service and serves on the End-User Services Task Force. She speaks and conducts workshops on integrating online and optical disc end-user reference services and is researching the impact and use of computer searching services in secondary schools.

Mara R. Saule is instruction coordinator in the reference department of the Bailey/Howe Library at the University of Vermont, Burlington, VT. She serves on the End-User Services Task Force and as public services coordinator for the implementation of the NOTIS integrated online library system. She is also optical product review editor for the journal *CD-ROM Librarian.*